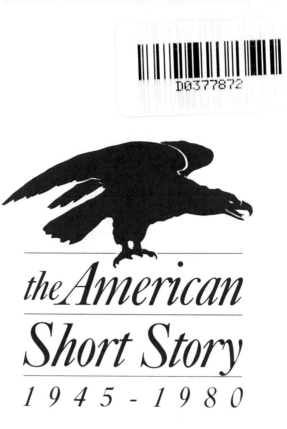

the American Short Story
1945 - 1980

A CRITICAL HISTORY

TWAYNE'S CRITICAL HISTORY
OF THE SHORT STORY

William Peden, General Editor
University of Missouri-Columbia

The American Short Story, 1850—1900
   Donald Crowley, University of Missouri-Columbia

The American Short Story, 1900—1945
   Philip Stevick, Temple University

The American Short Story, 1945—1980
   Gordon Weaver, Oklahoma State University

The British Short Story, 1890—1945
   Joseph M. Flora, University of North Carolina-Chapel Hill

The British Short Story, 1945—1980
   Dennis Vannatta, University of Arkansas-Little Rock

The Irish Short Story
   James Kilroy, Vanderbilt University

The Latin American Short Story
   Margaret Sayers Peden, University of Missouri-Columbia

the American Short Story
1945 - 1980

A CRITICAL HISTORY

❧

Gordon Weaver, Editor

Twayne Publishers

The American Short Story
1945—1980:
A Critical History

Copyright © 1983 by G. K. Hall & Company

All Rights Reserved

Published in 1983 by Twayne Publishers
A Division of G. K. Hall & Company
70 Lincoln Street, Boston, Massachusetts 02111

Printed on permanent/durable
acid-free paper and bound in
the United States of America

First Paperback Edition, August 1984

Book design and production
by Barbara Anderson

Typeset in 11 pt. Perpetua
by Compset, Inc. of Beverly, MA

Library of Congress Cataloging in Publication Data

Main entry under title:

The American short story, 1945—1980.

(Twayne's critical history of the short story)
Bibliography: p 111.
Includes index.
1. Short stories, America—History and criticism.
2. American fiction—20th century—History and criticism.
I. Weaver, Gordon.   II. Series.
PS374.S5A37   1983   813'.01'09   82-23423
ISBN 0-8057-9350-X
ISBN 0-8057-9355-0 (Pbk.)

Contents

Chronology

1945 President Franklin D. Roosevelt dies in Warm Springs, Georgia, April 12.

End of World War II: Germany surrenders to the Allies on May 8; Japan surrenders on August 14.

William March, *Trial Balance: Collected Short Stories* (contains stories from two earlier collections and previously uncollected work published after 1940).

James Thurber, *The Thurber Carnival* (contains stories from four earlier collections and previously uncollected pieces).

1946 Kay Boyle, *Thirty Stories* (contains stories from three earlier collections and previously uncollected stories including thirteen published in or after 1940).

Wilbur Daniel Steele, *The Best Short Stories of Wilbur Daniel Steele* (stories from five collections published between 1918 and 1926).

Edmund Wilson's *Memoirs of Hecate County* suppressed by New York State Court of Special Sessions. Reissued in 1959.

1949 Shirley Jackson, *The Lottery, or the Adventures of James Harris.* The title story, originally published in *The New Yorker,* is said to have elicited the largest reader response in the history of that magazine.

William Faulkner receives the Nobel Prize.

1950 Korean War begins, June 25.

William Faulkner, *Collected Stories* (contains stories from three earlier collections and several previously uncollected stories).

William Carlos Williams, *Make Light of It: Collected Stories* (contains stories from two earlier collections, previously uncollected stories, and thirteen previously unpublished pieces).

1952 *Paris Review* founded, with offices in Paris and New York. *Best Stories from the Paris Review,* with an introduction by William Styron, published in 1959.

1953 End of the Korean War.
John Cheever's first major collection, *The Enormous Radio and Other Stories* (preceded in 1943 by *The Way Some People Live*).
J. D. Salinger, *Nine Stories.*

1954 Ernest Hemingway receives the Nobel Prize.

1957 Isaac Bashevis Singer's first collection, *Gimpel the Fool and Other Stories.*
Bernard Malamud's first collection, *The Magic Barrel,* wins the National Book Award.
Demise of *Collier's Magazine.*

1959 Philip Roth's first book, *Goodbye, Columbus and Five Short Stories,* wins the National Book Award.

1960 *Story* revived under the editorship of Whit and Hallie Burnett (originally founded in Vienna by Whit Burnett and Martha Foley).
Conrad Aiken, *The Collected Short Stories of Conrad Aiken* (contains stories from three earlier collections and several previously uncollected stories).
Death of Richard Wright. His *Eight Men* is published the following year.

1961 Arrival of the first American support troops in Vietnam.
Death of Ernest Hemingway, in Idaho, from a self-inflicted gunshot wound.
Death of James Thurber.

1962 Death of William Faulkner, in Oxford, Mississippi.

1963 President John F. Kennedy assassinated in Dallas.

1964 Death of Flannery O'Connor.

1965 Katherine Anne Porter's *Collected Short Stories* wins the National Book Award.
Fifty Best American Short Stories 1915—1965; edited by Martha Foley from the annual *Best* series begun in 1915 under the editorship of Edward J. O'Brien.

1967   Death of Langston Hughes.

1968   Senator Robert F. Kennedy assassinated in Los Angeles.
The Reverend Dr. Martin Luther King assassinated in Memphis.

1969   *Collected Stories of Jean Stafford,* published posthumously, wins the Pulitzer Prize.
Demise of the *Saturday Evening Post.*

1970   *Fifty Years of the American Short Story,* selected by William Abrahams from the annual O. Henry Awards volumes; edited successively by Blanche Colton Williams, Harry Hansen, Herschel Brickell, and others.
Death of John O'Hara.

1971   *The Complete Stories of Flannery O'Connor.*

1972   Hemingway's *The Nick Adams Stories,* selected from earlier collections and including eight previously unpublished stories and sketches.

1973   United States withdraws from Vietnam.

1974   Watergate scandal and the resignation of President Nixon.

1975   Fiftieth anniversary of *The New Yorker.*

1978   *The Stories of John Cheever.*

1980   Ronald Reagan inaugurated as the fortieth President of the United States.
The Collected Stories of Eudora Welty.

Introduction

As the essays in this book demonstrate, the development of the American short story between 1945 and 1980 exhibits a gradual but ultimately clear movement in two distinct directions with respect to form. On one hand, American writers of serious literary short fiction continued to work within the traditional formal conventions established over the previous century, consolidating and refining the techniques of expression we associate with American masters as far back as Poe and Hawthorne, enriched by the influence of foreign practitioners such as Chekhov and Joyce. On the other hand, very recent contemporaries—perhaps the best example discussed hereafter is Donald Barthelme—indulged in various degrees of formal experimentation and innovation that derive perhaps as much from the impact of post-World War II cultural history as they do from earlier influential literary models. Kafka and Borges, in our century, come to mind, and one can cite fiction as early as Sterne in our novel tradition.

The short story is a very young literary form compared with poetry or even its narrative antecedent, the novel. Poetry's sources for our culture are classical; the novel comes to us from England and Europe. The short story is not only a relatively new genre—perhaps one hundred and seventy-five years in its modern tradition—it is a distinctly American literary phenomenon, despite important non-native influences. It would be presumptuous to declare emphatically that the form's future shape will be traditional or otherwise; the American short story remains dynamic in its esthetic character, flexible and varied, yet still recognizably what it has been, a vital mode of literary expression, continuously evolving toward the limits of its possibilities.

Jeffrey Walker finds that authors writing in the aftermath of World War II, many of whom began their literary careers before or during the war, continued to use the genre as a vehicle for thoughtful depiction and analysis of American social manners, mores, and morality. The stories of John O'Hara, written both then and after a long hiatus during which he wrote his massive novels of manners, can be used as an index to the particular social texture of both prewar and postwar America.

The American writers treated in the following essays use the short story as a lens to view a society within a narrow frame, but close up, magnified to reveal telling detail. This is true of John O'Hara and other *New Yorker* authors then and today; of regionalists such as Peter Taylor, Eudora Welty, and Flannery O'Connor, writing out of the American South in this era; of writers from the American West (Wallace Stegner, William Saroyan); and of those defined not so much by region as by class (Auchincloss), race (Langston Hughes), or even vocation (J. F. Powers).

The story of manners, discussed by Walker, appeared consistently over the years scrutinized here. We note also that a purely regional focus diminished, perhaps due to our increasing cultural homogeneity thanks to geographic mobility and the ubiquity of electronic media after World War II. Finally, many of the authors discussed by E. P. Walkiewicz (John Cheever, R. V. Cassill, William Goyen, Jesse Stuart, I. B. Singer) used the form for the depiction and moral analysis of American society and its constituent groups, whatever other ends their stories may serve.

As a primary, or even a very significant function of the genre, American society per se seems of less interest to most of the writers discussed by James C. Robison. Because the subjects treated by contemporary writers come from their own experience, however, the short story continues to provide a view of the society in which the reader lives.

Like the genre itself, the themes, explicit or implicit, are distinctly American. There are more moral questions than moral conclusions, an attitude that can be traced to the dark Puritan consciousness of Nathaniel Hawthorne. The writers discussed in these essays project two overlapping fields of vision, two separate angles of scope that are almost always in some degree of conflict: society, and the individual's place in and relationship to that society. In American culture, itself so historically new as yet to be declaring its shape and texture (one might pause and remember that Roman legions occupied Britain longer than Western culture has existed in the New World), the cult of individualism has made one's relationship to that culture obscure, even mysterious, as it is closely and profoundly considered by short stories. Thus the themes of individual isolation and alienation repeatedly emerge from the works discussed. In addition to their concern with individuation of psychology and soul, the authors hold up society itself to severe moral scrutiny.

• • •

Hortense Calisher's New Yorkers, the Glass family in J. D. Salinger's stories, James T. Farrell's urban Irish, Wiliam Humphrey's "Texahomans," Langston Hughes's blacks (all surveyed by Jeffrey Walker) are people isolated by class, caste, region, or tortured temperament, from a fulfilling sense of belonging. As they search for identity or quarrel with inadequate social and moral personas imposed on them by their American experience, these characters confront a national culture itself as morally inexplicable or unacceptable as the fictional situations in which they find themselves.

E. P. Walkiewicz examines these themes in short fiction published between 1957 and 1968: John Updike dramatizes the moral complexity that is the modern social institution of marriage on the sensitive planes of spiritual and esthetic sensibility; W. H. Gass's Midwesterners wither on the dry vine of moral sterility in America's heartland; Bernard Malamud's urban Jews, stripped of their Old World religious identities, are torn between a dead or dying tradition and New World chaos; Flannery O'Connor's Deep South grotesques act out a bizarre symbolism for an orthodox Christianity that survives only in the gothic outlines of Bible Belt fundamentalism.

James C. Robison's study of our most recent authors reveals Joyce Carol Oates, Guy Davenport, James Alan McPherson, Leonard Michaels, Daniel Curley, and Barry Targan, among others, challenging traditional esthetic conventions in an effort to find some moral base in society in general or groups within it on which contemporary characters can mount and articulate a vision of individual identity and culture. These authors seek bases for the continuity of human existence itself.

The title story of Shirley Ann Grau's *The Black Prince and Other Stories* (1954) exhibits another confrontation with the Deep South's racial dilemma. It is reminiscent of the work of numerous earlier regional authors, but it anticipates the emerging American social and moral concern that erupted in the turbulence of Little Rock, Selma, and other highwater marks of this cultural preoccupation that, along with the Vietnam conflict, dominated the 1960s. The surface of Grau's story never directly touches on racial segregation, which deeply troubled moral philosophers and social reformers alike for so long, but that phenomenon is implicitly pervasive in her story. It is the evident concern and admiration for what has come to be called black consciousness, the vitality of the life force manifest in black experience that animates the fiction. Much of what has come to be articulated as valuable in black America—its deeply rooted human impulses and responses, quite mythically sensual and sexual in Grau's story—is at the fore in this seemingly melodramatic tale. The story is couched in the traditional tone and outline of myth, and Grau's Black Prince is a traditional demonic hero. "The Black Prince" is at one and the same time a traditionally regional slice of life and an almost prophetic projection of attitudes and beliefs that were to come to popular national consciousness over the next several years.

By the time of Bruce J. Friedman's *Black Angels* (1966) and James Alan McPherson's *Hue and Cry* (1969), the explosive revolution of black awareness, black politics, and black culture as significant elements in the larger society are commonplaces, dramatized as such in American short fiction.

William H. Gass's *In the Heart of the Heart of the Country*, published in 1968, contains several traditional stories that might be called primarily regional evocations of manners, not dramatically different from the story of manners executed with such particularity over the whole period by Louis Auchincloss or John O'Hara. Gass's title story, a long and almost plotless meditation on his life by a narrator in a state of moral and emotional stasis, exhibits formal qualities that seem especially appropriate to the story's mood; the narrator's severe dissociation from self and culture is rendered in his trivial response to the land about him, a rural wasteland, and by his disjointed references to the past that has brought him to this condition of paralyzed isolation.

In "The Black Prince," Grau's segregated Negroes inhabit a world that is fully realized, a geography that imitates a real world of history and sociology. In "In the Heart of the Heart of the Country," Gass brings his reader to a milieu that is still recognizably the American Midwest, but that is now more memory than substance. The subject of the story is the American psyche turning on itself, as morally intense in its painful introspection as it is imprecise in its attempt at moral definition. If Grau's story can be said to anticipate what was to come with respect to the race "problem," Gass's can be seen as depicting the national psychology now out of touch with its traditional points of reference—history, region, fellow citizen—groping toward an as yet indistinct framework on which to reconstruct a new, life-giving moral perception of human experience in "post-modern" America.

Thus as we move in time from Grau's fiction to that of Gass, we observe a marked breakdown in traditional American idealism, whether the focus is race relations or the need for love. This is reflected in deviations from traditional short story form, and is even more pronounced in Gass's later work, which all but abandons correspondence to earlier structure and attempts to enhance its meaning by its altered shape.

In the three collections of stories by Raymond Carver published between 1976 and 1980, traditional form persists, but only minimally. Carver treats the story as epiphany, his brutally spare slices of life so thin as barely to establish viable contexts for their moments of ironic statement or awareness. Another way of viewing Carver's work is that his economy of words is a statement equally as severe as Gass's, to the effect that the scope of the perceivable world, conventionally understood as history and community, has withered to a degree that will not permit articulate consciousness. Carver's characters are burned out by love, by drink, and by the paralyzing impact of contemporary history since World War II—atomic warfare and the specter of global nuclear holocaust, the Korean stalemate and the Cold War, Vietnam, the Kennedy years that ended in assassination, racial turmoil, the popularization of drugs, record divorce rates, Watergate, economic stagnation . . . Raymond Carver is not an experimental writer in the same category as the later William Gass, Guy Davenport, or Donald Barthelme, but his short stories do take traditional form to an extremity that begins to constitute self-conscious desertion of established esthetics, despite reliance on authentic dialogue and realistic action.

•   •   •

What emerges from this spectrum is the idea of the contemporary American short story as an index of national consciousness. It takes up as its subjects, however obliquely (for no writers wish to think of themselves as dependent on a daily newspaper for the matter of fiction), the very events that dominate current consciousness. Our contemporary story *is* a historical artifact in and of itself, and in a sense that is by no means unimportant, the writers discussed herein are historians. This means they not only record our history, they anticipate and interpret it, not with an eye toward prediction or evaluation of trends, but for its moral revelation. Today's American short story is a vision, multifaceted as the numbers of its serious practitioners, of American life. It focuses on what it means to be human, and thus becomes an agent of perception with the capacity for influencing moral action in America today.

The short story is well adapted to the development of that vision. As traditional social structures and attitudes crumble, as moral definitions are challenged by the hard realities of American experience in the aftermath of World War II, forms alter to accommodate new visions or old ones in a state of flux. The neat sequence of chronological narration gives way to fragmentation and distortion; the rounded depiction of milieu and character is reduced to a narrow—though no less telling—slice or a vague presence; language and our assumptions about its properties and capacities come under scrutiny.

At the extreme, an author's irony may be so blatant (as with Barthelme or Davenport) as to defy the assumption that either language or the genre can adequately comprehend or contain the seemingly endless variety of contemporary consciousness. This can be seen in several of the stories in Russell Banks's *The New World: Tales* (1978), in which historical characters are dramatized in an effort (perhaps to meet a human need) to re-endow "dead" history with new life transmitted back to the past from the present.

What emerges from the reflection of American history and social upheaval is the inescapable fact that a formal definition of the genre has yet to be articulated. Indeed, the subjects themselves seem to have brought about its division into two formal directions, traditional and experimental (or innovative).

· · ·

A short story is only subjectively "short," and what one reader might be able to concentrate on fully at a single sitting (to recall Poe's early definition) could well prove too long for another or not long enough for yet another. If short stories are short, at least shorter than novels, we cannot say just how short they must be, and the work surveyed in the following essays runs the gamut from brief epiphany to long narrative. A purely quantitative scale, exactly distinguishing short story from novel (or novella, to complicate matters) is not possible.

The concept of persona, or voice, is at least a bit more helpful. Every fiction (novel or story) is told by a fictional persona; this is one means of distinguishing it from nonfiction in which the voice is assumed to be that of the author. Although in fiction there may be a first-person narrator who refers to himself or herself as being the author, the reader makes the assumption that this is a device—the persona is always the mask that word's Greek root signifies.

In the traditional story, there is no attempt to confuse the reader as to this distinction. This practice, still dominant, as the authors surveyed here demonstrate, does not call into question the difference between fiction and reality. The experimental mode, however, which has been used more and more in the most recent decade, brings up precisely that question. For example, in self-reflexive fiction, an esthetic assumption appears to be that the work is as real as any other phenomenon in the perceptual and material world, and that fiction is as valid an experience as any other. Perhaps a more basic assumption of such experiments is that language itself is as real as the world it has been heretofore understood only to symbolize.

This contention came into being out of the historical experience since World War II, in which moral and social orders were perceived as bankrupt, as was the language customary to understanding (or reforming or casting aside) them. A new consciousness, perhaps in some sense even a new language, was required to fathom and cope with this situation. Hence a new fiction (or art of whatever sort) was required.

It is also true that any fiction is a statement, however pessimistic or nihilistic about the reality it invokes, that implies, if not some conceivable alternative to the way things are, at least a hypothetical norm or ideal against which its moral criticism can be dramatized. In the end, we have only our language and the conventions of the genre (persona being just a formal feature of fiction), and authors can choose from a range of possibilities that includes taking the conventions as our tradition has transmitted them or altering them to the point at which communication ceases.

One may refer directly to oneself as author, by name, but it does not affect the fact that fiction must have a persona. One can point to the ironic meanings of words in a particular context—in the same sense that one indicates the rhythmic dimension of words in the context of a poem—but words will continue to have significance with respect to the real world. A writer can fragment, distort, or obscure the narrative sequence, but fiction will remain nevertheless narrative, however much of its coherence relies on the reader's reconstruction of it. Thus the distinction between traditional and experimen tal stories is more surface than substance, and literary experiment, with its roots traceable back to the very sources of our novelistic tradition in the eighteenth century (one thinks again of Sterne), has its own conventions. The history of the short story is a brief one, traceable only to the early nineteenth century in America, and one must conclude that its formal characteristics are in an early, rather than a definitive stage of development.

• • •

As a commercial enterprise, short stories are a poor speculative venture at best; a mass market for them has all but disappeared. The impact of electronic media and the decline in the numbers of general magazine formats are often cited as among the chief causes; exceptions such as *The New Yorker* and a few other survivors are notable primarily because they *are* exceptions. Unless the author of short stories has a reputation previously established by commercial success with the novel or augmented by the celebrity of television or film, there is little hope of earning a living by practicing the craft.

The interest of large commercial publishing houses in short-story collections (or anthologies) is in equivalent decline. The successful novelist or the writer with a reputation built over several decades (John Cheever, for example, or Peter Taylor) may be assured of the publication of his collected stories, but younger, uncelebrated authors must look elsewhere for an audience.

This void has been filled to a great extent by the profusion of "small" literary magazines. Some of them are well established by university sponsorship and secure now by the sheer fact of survival over many years, although it often seems that as many cease publication each year as are founded. Little magazines have sprung into being in response to the drying up of publishing outlets over the past twenty years. Some of them demonstrate a tendency toward specialization, announcing hard policies with respect to traditional versus experimental writing, or espousing one or another extraliterary policy (gay, black, feminist, etc.) through the vehicle of the short story (and poetry and essay). There are, then, diverse audiences for the short story, all of them small; thus one might be inclined to assume that the extent to which the genre has any real potential for influence on either American policies or sensibility is questionable. At the worst, it might appear that the situation affecting publication of short stories in America presages a medium less and less able to find an audience. Yet it is clear that, nurtured in large part by academia, there is a vigorous creative impulse in our culture that will not be denied, and that prophecies of the death of the short story are as inaccurate as those that have been made about the novel. There is no reason to believe, given our tradition, that serious writers have broken off the practice of the craft because either financial reward was unlikely or appreciative audiences minuscule. There is every reason to believe, ultimately, that the future of the American short story will be as richly productive as it has ever been, and no reason to think—recognizing that art, unlike technology, is not subject to "progress"—that the quality of achievement to be expected is likely to diminish.

$$\bullet \quad \bullet \quad \bullet$$

It would be tempting to pronounce definitive judgment on the relative merits of the writers treated in these essays, to rank them as to first, second, or third order of excellence. The critical evaluations of the authors of the three essays are implicit, reflected in terms of the detail and space devoted to an individual writer (although this is also reflective of relative quantity of work), where it is not explicit. We should avoid a commonplace tendency of our culture to declare a "best" or "top ten" when it comes to serious and accomplished literary art. Such sweeping assessments are doubtless easy if we talk of competitive sports or commodities valued in dollars. It is quite otherwise with art, and the authors referred to herein are artists. It is also more difficult to assess the literary achievement of living and recently deceased writers than it is to know the worth of the long-dead, whose creations are fixed and limited for our deliberation.

One premise operative in this book was that only authors of collections of stories would be considered; those whose work through 1980 was published only in periodicals were thus eliminated. Furthermore, although there are a very few (but significant) exceptions, only authors of two or more collections were considered to have produced a canon of sufficient volume to justify consideration.

The reader will notice that, in some instances, reference is quite naturally made to stories published by an individual (John Cheever, for example) prior to 1945; this is for the purposes of coherence and comprehensiveness. Also, some writers (Doris Betts is one) whose collections of stories have appeared at relatively regular intervals over the course of the last thirty-five years are discussed in all three essays. Finally, while in some cases an author's work is restricted to discussion in only one of the essays (see Robison's treatment of Daniel Curley), reference is also made to work produced in a period covered in another essay; this reflects the period in which a writer's major work, or the vast majority of work, was published in collected form. The productivity of short-story writers does not fit exactly, sometimes not even neatly, in arbitrary chronologies.

It is sufficient to say that this study demonstrates that the genre is alive and well, dynamic, as vital and viable a form of literary expression as it has ever been; reports of its demise are not only premature, they are ludicrous.

The selected bibliography of short-story collections gives an indication of just how many stories have been brought, and are being brought, to readers in the last three and one-half decades. They still almost always appear first in commercial and literary magazines, and while publishers are not eager to bring out collections due to the rare chance of making a profit, American university presses and small presses have increasingly chosen to handle them. In addition to the collections listed in the bibliography, the interested reader should consult the *Small Press Record of Books in Print,* 10th edition (Paradise, Calif., 1981—82), edited by Len Fulton and Ellen Ferber, for the most recent complete record of the output of America's small presses.

Of course, the editor accepts the blame for errors or serious omissions in this study, while crediting Jeffrey Walker, E. P. Walkiewicz, and James C. Robison for their achievement and the voluminous reading and research it entailed to produce their essays. The research assistance of William Shute is also greatly appreciated.

Gordon Weaver

Oklahoma State University

1945—1956:
POST-WORLD WAR II
MANNERS AND MORES

The history of the American short story in the decade following the Second World War was not marked by radical changes or startling breakthroughs in style or subject matter. What did occur was a movement toward developing a literature that would mirror the intricacies of life in postwar America. No longer convinced that the journalistic technique that characterized fiction of the depression years was sufficient to interpret contemporary life, and not yet ready to initiate experimental modes that would gain popularity in the early 1960s, the writers of the late 1940s and early 1950s concentrated on the story of manners, a tradition that has characterized the short story since Henry James.

Witty and often satiric, these sketches chronicled the lives of ordinary people. Unlike the naturalists of the 1930s, however, who emphasized broad social issues, writers probed with uncanny insight the manners and mores of the upper, lower, and middle classes; the bedroom, barroom, and drawing room; the city, suburbs, and country. Their stories revealed the inner tensions and conflicts between parents and children, husbands and wives, friends and lovers. They treated such diverse and complex topics as childhood, alienation, old age, disillusionment, and the eternal search for one's identity.

Many writers in this period had published collections of stories before the war and were caught up in the trends developing in the postwar era. John O'Hara, for example, was not only a prolific author in the 1930s and early 1940s, during which time he published five collections, but also in the 1960s when six volumes of his work appeared. The same can be said for James T. Farrell, Eudora Welty, and William Saroyan. Some, like Tennessee Williams and Truman Capote, who as young men began their careers after the war, gained their measure of fame in the 1960s and 1970s. The *New Yorker* cadre of writers, their stories marked by urbanity and wit, and the members of the Southern renaissance, who found fascination in the sometimes grotesque incongruities of character and setting, tended to produce the largest quantity of fiction in the period. Short-story masters such as James A. Michener and Ray Bradbury continued their output in a wide range of fictional areas.

To isolate these writers into stylistic, thematic, or geographic schools, however, would be a mistake. What does characterize them as part of a common literary tradition is their ability to turn tales of local color and social behavior—stories of manners—into metaphors of the American experience.

•   •   •

A major writer in this tradition is John O'Hara (1905—1970). O'Hara is remarkable in the history of American short-story writers because his career spans five decades and includes twelve collections, plus an anthology of his earlier work. What is even more remarkable is that these collections were published in two different eras, 1935 to 1947, and 1960 to 1972. Although the later stories are probably the best, the earlier tales are characteristic of many of the qualities that were his trademark. Of the five volumes published in the first period, three appeared before the Second World War: *The Doctor's Son and Other Stories* (1935), *Files on Parade* (1939), and *Pal Joey* (1940). Two came out in postwar America: *Pipe Night* (1945) and *Hellbox* (1947).

O'Hara's stories of manners are representative of the style of living exemplified in this period; yet he treats people and their problems in a fashion that is unique. His world is an amoral one, one in which the guilty are not always punished or the innocent always allowed to prevail. The forces of life, whether good or evil, affect everyone, regardless of social position. In fact, social status itself is the motivating factor in many of his stories. O'Hara's method of storytelling borders on the detached fashion of merely reporting the events that occur in the lives of his characters. There is little emphasis on providing psychological insight into motives or methods. The thirty-one stories in *Pipe Night* illustrate this technique.

"Walter T. Carriman," the opening story, narrated by a first-person observer, turns into a "tribute" to his friend, "everybody's friend, Walter T. Carriman." The irony, of course, is the relatively little information the narrator possesses about Carriman's life. He makes this clear in several ways. First, he tells the reader he will report "merely" what he, as one of Carriman's friends, knows about Walter. Therefore he will present "only certain 'highlights'" of his own "arbitrary choosing," leaving others to "elaborate upon or extend these words." Second, in his picture of Walter, the narrator displays a habit for qualifying all his information: "Not having been surrounded in his childhood by great riches, which have been known to disappear overnight . . . Walter, on the other hand, was not raised in poverty and squalor, the details of which can . . . prove equally boresome." Elsewhere in his portrait, the narrator admits that while as a boy, "Walter had been fond of baseball," his participation in sports did not continue "owing to defective vision," and later to training rules that "proved irksome to a lad of Walter's spirit. . . . (The truth is that Walter took his first cigarette at the age of fourteen and from then on was a rather heavy smoker)." Walter, "on the intellectual side," was "somewhere between the studious and the casual." Details like this, as well as the facts of Walter's wandering from job to job, suggest that the narrator's eulogy is not only unconvincing in its sincerity, but consistent in its depiction of a banal and rather lifeless personality.

Not all of O'Hara's characters, however, are banal; rather they are people who survive the bleakness of their isolation. O'Hara makes no attempt to communicate his characters' inner souls; yet they are vividly portrayed as empty people who seek to escape the quiet desperation of routine. Story after story reveals this theme. In "Too Young," a girl uses her affair with a motorcycle cop to fulfill her physical needs; in "Free," a California woman travels all the way to New York for a shopping spree, but spends her time daydreaming about an affair she would like to have but never will; in "Can You Carry Me?" a Hollywood actress verbally abuses a magazine editor because of a story he printed about her, but ends up going to bed with him; in "Nothing Missing," a man just released from prison enters a bookstore to stare at a clerk—just to stare, never to talk; in "A Purchase of Some Golf Clubs," an off-duty mechanic sitting in a bar buys a set of golf clubs from a girl who needs the money to free her husband from jail. In almost all of O'Hara's early stories, nothing much "happens," inner psyches are seldom revealed, and resolutions to characters' problems are never really achieved. In every case, he portrays the everyday affairs of ordinary people in a manner that exposes their failures.

As the author of over three hundred short stories, O'Hara is effective in his vignettes of contemporary manners if only because of the power of redundancy; characters and scenes appear again and again. He has almost made a genre of these sketches, and while the reader may wish for more variety, few can argue with the success of his efforts in *Pipe Night, Hellbox,* and the earlier collections. O'Hara does not have the technical range of other writers, but what he does, he does well. He exposes the worst side of human beings—their greed, stupidity, crassness, and selfishness—and convinces the reader that people cannot escape themselves.

• • •

O'Hara was the first of a group of writers who contributed to a literary phenomenon that was to characterize the story of manners in postwar America. Since 1925, *The New Yorker* magazine had been publishing what it considered the best short stories in the country. Most of these were similar in that they relied on brief anecdotes or autobiographical sketches written in a sophisticated style and dealing with contemporary behavior of ordinary people.

Edward Newhouse (1911—   ), for example, like O'Hara, has been a regular contributor. In the six years following the war, Newhouse published two collections of short fiction: *The Iron Chain* (1946) and *Many Are Called: Forty-Two Short Stories* (1951). All but four of the twenty-one stories in the first volume and three of the forty-two in the second appeared in *The New Yorker,* where for years Newhouse was a staff member. He followed what many have called the *New Yorker* formula with stories that are brief character sketches made memorable by their portrayal of cosmopolitan manners and mores rather than by vivid, thoughtful studies of motives and psyches. In some ways, these works are like the magazine's cartoons, with captions that run for half a page instead of one line. Much as O'Hara provides photographic portraits, Newhouse's sketches capture not only the feel of conversation, but ambiance of place.

In "A Gorgeous Number," from *The Iron Chain,* Newhouse describes in five pages a moment in the life of Miss Mae Garvey, a young girl waiting in Jake's Third Avenue saloon for her boyfriend. In her conversation with Jake, she recounts the other men who have courted her, and while sitting there she meets Major Thomas Driscoll, a midget. At the Major's overtures, Miss Garvey breaks into a fit of laughter, and the story ends with him stomping out of the bar. Nothing substantial happens, but the conversation reveals Newhouse's ability to record the vernacular and the habits of a segment of New York society. The other stories in the collection (each averaging ten pages) report similar scenes. Readers can identify with the characters because they are people like themselves captured in moments that show how the commonplace can be both lively and exciting.

• • •

Like his *New Yorker* colleague Edward Newhouse, John McNulty (1895—1956) describes the milieu of Third Avenue and the people who frequent its establishments. The best way to describe McNulty's works is to accept his definition in the foreword to *A Man Gets Around* (1951): they are "casuals"; stories "about people here and there and about happenings in New York, N.Y." In this collection, as well as in the earlier *Third Avenue, New York* (1946), McNulty's ear for the nuances of speech and his appreciation of the vitality of life are evident. His stories, including those in *My Son Johnny* (1955) and *The World of John McNulty* (1957) are usually brief, but they treat the commonplace with gusto and the insignificant with originality. In the dedication to *The World of John McNulty,* published posthumously, James Thurber praises McNulty's "unflagging comic spirit." Although not an innovator in the development of the American short story, his stories are characteristic of the fiction about New York City published in the late 1940s and early 1950s.

• • •

A writer of much greater achievement than McNulty who also uses New York City as her milieu is Hortense Calisher (1911—   ). In *In the Absence of Angels* (1951), she describes New Yorkers as a weary lot, beset by the problems of living in a world inhospitable to innocence. They are dreamers and failures, rejects who fail because of their human frailty, their absence of grace, and their inability to establish lasting relationships with the people with whom they work, live, and love.

The title story reflects this failure. The first-person narrator describes the barrenness of her life. She recalls the friends of her youth, her sick mother, and the existence that with hindsight seems to have been a harbinger of her present life, one filled with despair. In her thoughts, she concludes, "finally, that there is no place for people like us, that the middle ground is for angels, not for men. But there is a place. For in the absence of angels and arbiters from a world of light, men and women must take their place."

Many of the other stories echo this theme. Two, "A Box of Ginger" and "The Watchers," recount the youth of Hester Elkin and her response to the death of her grandmother. The chief effect Calisher achieves is failure of the family members because of their inability to share their feelings. Each is isolated by generation, insularity, and unwillingness to resolve the tensions that all of them ironically create and propagate. In "The Woman Who Was Everybody," Miss Abel, who wears "one of the two dresses of the daily requisite black," peers out her window and imagines people like herself asking, "Do you suppose . . . is there anything to be made of me?" She not only seeks a job, but also engages in a depressing affair with a "boy, Max," who would visit and in the "muffled clingings of love-making . . . try again to build up some dark mutual core of unalienable wholeness." Finally, she repeats what she already knows: she is one of the rejected. Equally hopeless are the night riders in the "Night Riders of Northville" who spend their life commuting from home to office and from bar to bar, listening to the sameness of the "ratchety-slat of the pinball machine," than which there is "no more aimless sound in the world."

Calisher's stories are effective not only because of her unremitting portraits of lost souls, but also because of her method of portraying character and place. All of her people are reflections of the places in which they exist. The skies are gray, the trees are gray, the characters and their lives are gray. Every action and response takes place in a middle world in which choices are never clear, and despair, alienation, and confusion reign. These people are never able to escape from this world, because neither they nor the society to which they belong is capable of establishing a lasting set of values. Like Edith Wharton, whose novels of New York manners are compassionate yet hopeless accounts of the human condition, Calisher portrays her world with insight and understanding.

•   •   •

Louis Auchincloss (1917—   ) creates quite a different fictional world. His stories are concerned almost exclusively with the upper crust of American society: lawyers, business titans, patrons of the arts. In his two collections published in the early 1950s, *The Injustice Collectors* (1950) and *The Romantic Egoists: A Reflection in Eight Minutes* (1954), Auchincloss reports on the contemporary manners of the Eastern seaboard establishment. *The Injustice Collectors* contains eight stories chronicling the lives of people who are "looking for injustice, even in a friendly world, because they suffer from a hidden need to feel that this world has wronged them." In "Greg's Peg," for instance, Auchincloss reveals how social pressure can destroy people. Gregory Bakewell, a misfit in his social class, attempts to gain acceptance by trying to mold his personality to fit the crowd with whom he associates. His efforts, however, are pathetic as he transforms himself into a caricature of the summer colony type. Rebuffed, his company no longer desired, he leaves Anchor Harbor and eventually dies of a heart attack. Auchincloss is successful in rendering the attitudes of Eastern society in this story because he reveals, in more depth than Newhouse, the motives and uncertainties of his characters. Much like Edith Wharton and Henry James, Auchincloss captures the pulse and rhythm of people who pressure themselves to survive in a world that often rebuffs such attempts. These people are deluded into thinking that they must conform: as characters they fall victim to their own insecurities.

The eight stories of the *The Romantic Egoists* follow a similar pattern. "The Fortune of Arleus Kane" details the fortunes and misfortunes of Kane as he makes aborted attempts to enter politics; "Wally" reveals the battle for position in a naval training camp; "The Legends of Henry Everett" exposes the life of a lawyer who is treated with reverence at court and like an "un-housetrained puppy" at home.

All are examples of Auchincloss's technique of using a first-person narrator, and all reveal observers who learn what Henry Everett concludes in his speech to the bar association: ". . . it is one thing to know or even suspect that one knows nothing and quite another to *believe* in nothing—." In this context, Auchincloss's characters are romantic egoists: few believe in anything. He reveals that the ennui and sense of desolation and loneliness usually associated with the middle class is also very much a part of the world of the rich. Whether his setting is a naval base or a lawyer's office, Auchincloss is a master technician who reports the pathos of the upper class.

. . .

Another writer for *The New Yorker* whose best work appeared in the postwar era is Mary McCarthy (1912—   ). Unlike O'Hara, who presented an external view of motives (revealing largely what they did and the effect on others, rather than why they did it) McCarthy investigates her characters' psyches to analyze the reasons underlying their actions. Tailored to reveal many of her own experiences, McCarthy's stories are about incidents in the lives of young women, either her favorite character, Margaret Sargent, or an unnamed "she." In all cases, the stories go beyond O'Hara's photographic realism to provide readers with an inside view of a woman who seeks her own identity and will do whatever is necessary to achieve her ends.

McCarthy objectively exposes the foibles and follies of her young heroines, never by telling us about them, but by showing them in action. Because their portraits are presented dramatically, we come to know their thoughts and the reasons behind what they do. In "Cruel and Barbarous Treatment," collected in *The Company She Keeps* (1942), the reader learns about a young woman who is having an affair and thinking about divorce with the same sense of exhilaration she felt at the time of her engagement. At the beginning of the story, McCarthy tells us that the young wife could "not bear to hurt her husband. She impressed this on the Young Man, on her confidantes, and finally on her husband himself." For her, however, the details are so exciting that she cannot escape what she sees as the glamor of becoming a "young divorcee." She proceeds with the self-centered confidence of one who knows all along that everything will turn out to be socially acceptable. She is not only conceited, but a snob.

This story typically depicts the society in which McCarthy's women roam, always anticipating some excitement, and oblivious to the danger of hurting anyone in the process, sometimes even themselves. Their coldness and lack of conscience mark them as independent as any women in contemporary fiction. The same types appear in McCarthy's next volume of stories, *Cast a Cold Eye* (1950). The title is revealing, for not only do the characters view their lives dispassionately, but the reader is aware of McCarthy's own cold eye in presenting these stories of social relationships. "The Weeds" analyzes the effect of separation on a woman who has left her husband; "Yonder Peasant, Who Is He?" concerns the responses of a young girl to her parents' deaths; "C. Y. E." reports events in a Catholic boarding school. All reveal the coldness of their central characters and form a satiric indictment of urban relationships.

. . .

Jean Stafford (1915—1979) is a writer and chronicler of manners in the McCarthy tradition. Her first and best collection, *Children Are Bored on Sunday* (1953), is diverse in range and subject. From "The Echo and the Nemesis," which describes Ramona Dunn, a terribly obese and pathetic girl who invents a mirror image of herself as a svelte twin sister, to the title story in which a young woman who comes home to New York feels socially insecure among those with whom she thinks she is intellectually inferior, Stafford provides a glimpse into a world characterized by the mildly aberrant to the grotesque. The orphaned Indian boy of "A Summer Day," the Mexican girl in "The Bleeding Heart," the Jewish doctor in "The Home Front," and the American girl in "A Winter's Tale" are characters who, despite their individual situations, have one thing in common: they are all alienated and lonely, living in a world in which anything horrible is possible and usually happens.

Stafford's grotesque world is depicted in "The Home Front." A lonely Jewish doctor, who administers aid to factory workers, has the misfortune of living in a boarding house run by an antisemitic landlady. When he befriends a cat, the landlady and her son kill it. In an unexpected climax, the doctor, dedicated to the saving of lives, kills the son's pet bird in retaliation. The doctor has assumed the cruelty of the environment in which he lives. This is what can happen, Stafford suggests here and in the other stories, when people find themselves in a world to which they are unable to adjust. The fault lies, of course, with a flaw in humanity, not with the environment itself. While some of Stafford's later stories are a bit more encouraging in their portrayal of contemporary life, her best ones suggest the personal agonies of alienation and loss.

· · ·

With *New Yorker* writers tending to be masters of comic satire in their chastisement of American manners, it is not surprising that J. F. Powers (1917—   ) has been published frequently in the magazine's pages. Although his stories are concerned with pastors, curates, and parishioners of the Catholic Church, they are not devoted to discussions of theological issues. They are instead brilliantly written comedies of manners using as their province the world of the church with its own intricate code of behavior. Powers's stories reveal the idiosyncratic and unspectacular in the daily lives of his characters and do so in a witty and ironic fashion that gives the tales practical significance.

While some readers might assume that stories peopled with church figures would deal with the good or evil nature of the characters portrayed, Powers's work presents his individuals as victims, often sympathetic and almost always comic, of the passions and petty jealousies that motivate human beings to action. His storytelling methods often help to soften some of those baser human traits he describes. "The Forks," for instance, from the first collection, *The Prince of Darkness and Other Stories* (1947), is representative of the techniques Powers uses to reveal the conflicts between curate and pastor. Monsignor Sweeney, a conservative and materialistic pastor who views his assistant, Father Eudex, as naive for believing that he should act like a Christian, tries to convince Father Eudex of the importance of appearances. He argues for the prudent, practical way of doing things, even going so far as to instruct him about what forks to use at mealtime. At the end of the story, a disillusioned Eudex is almost tempted to believe that the priesthood no longer has any real mission. Such conflicts characterize many of the works in *The Prince of Darkness*. Even the title story presents a priest whose pride and lack of any real religious conviction mark him as an anomaly to those who view the world of the church with unbiased idealism.

In Powers's second collection, *The Presence of Grace* (1956), most of the nine stories continue this theme. Powers's attention to detail and his use of viewpoint are especially noteworthy. Perhaps the best works in the collection are "Death of a Favorite" and "Defection of a Favorite," both narrated by the rectory cat, Fritz. The tone is ironic, and Powers once more is able to parry and thrust satirically through a series of incidents between assistant and pastor. This time, however, the spats are refereed by a cat. In "Defection of a Favorite," Fritz must contend with Father Burner, the same "prince of darkness" central to the earlier story. When Father Malt, the parish priest, slips on the ice and fractures his hip, Father Burner assumes command. Although less proud than before, Burner sees his chance to continue in that office. His new regime produces changes that prompt Fritz to observe that with "Father Burner running the rectory, it was going to be a hard, hard, and probably fatal winter for me." The winter turns out, however, to be fatal for Father Burner's ambition and not for Fritz. The assistant's careful plans backfire when Father Malt resumes his position. Through it all, at least from Fritz's perspective, Burner learns, with Fritz's "good company and constant example," to accept the setback "with grace."

In "A Losing Game," Father Fabre, the parish attendant, finds himself the loser in another of Powers's contests between curate and pastor. Father Fabre is a young man who dreams of doing great works at Trinity, but he soon comes to feel that his pastor is maneuvering against him. Because the story is told from Fabre's point of view, the reader sees the events as Fabre sees them, and quickly discovers that the game under way is being played only by the young assistant. The pastor is completely innocent, and in a series of comic confrontations, Fabre ends up merely frustrating himself and acting the fool.

Powers's stories succeed not only because of his technical expertise, but also because he is a master of comic satire. He has a feel for revealing the foibles of his characters, and with his insight and wit he lampoons many of their battles. In the process, Powers reveals much about the motives and complexities of ordinary men.

* * *

Equally adept at commenting on the American scene is Shirley Jackson (1919—1965). What has probably become the most frequently anthologized modern short story, "The Lottery," first appeared in *The New Yorker* and later was the title story of *The Lottery: or, The Adventures of James Harris* (1949). Few readers have failed to recognize the very real elements of human depravity in Jackson's story of the scapegoat on whom all the evils of the community are laid. In this respect, the story is a telling and chilling indictment of American society.

"The Lottery" opens with a realistic portrayal of small-town life. The characters are friendly, neighborly people preparing for an undescribed event that appears to be part of the town's tradition, gathering a pile of stones. This seems innocent enough until the climax of the story when realism is replaced by symbolism, and expectation turns into shock when the townspeople stone to death one of their own. This surprise ending, which contrasts everyday affairs with events that are more comfortably left alone, is an example of Jackson's ability to analyze the feelings and emotions of people caught up in outdated traditions and customs.

* * *

The stories of J. D. Salinger (1919—   ) present excellent examples of people trying to cope with the pressures created by social values and traditions. His novel, *The Catcher in the Rye* (1951), cemented his reputation as a commentator on the world of adolescents and misfits, but Salinger's short stories are also of importance.

Salinger's first collection, *Nine Stories* (1953), was selected from thirty stories published between 1940 and 1953. All but two ("Down at the Dinghy" and "De Daumier-Smith's Blue Period") appeared originally in *The New Yorker.* Like *Catcher,* the predominant theme is alienation, an alienation that usually ends in reconciliation, but in some cases, death. This sense of isolation is caused by several factors. In "Down at the Dinghy," racial prejudice is the issue when a young boy overhears the housekeeper call his father a "kike." He runs away to the family dinghy, but is finally coaxed home by his mother. Salinger's irony is evident here, for after all that the reader is led to believe about the boy's misery, it turns out that he was disturbed because he thought his father was being called a "kite."

Two other stories in the collection, "Just Before the War with the Eskimos" and "The Laughing Man," deal with broken love affairs, while two others reveal estrangement in marriage, "Uncle Wiggily in Connecticut" and "Pretty Mouth and Green My Eyes." The last is a particularly good example of Salinger's portrait of urban manners. A young executive places two telephone calls to his boss; in each, he wonders aloud as to the whereabouts of his wife. During both calls, she is in bed with the boss.

Although these tales of alienation in love are excellent, Salinger's finest works portray an isolation even more profound. "For Esmé—with Love and Squalor," perhaps his best story, recounts the crisis of a veteran who has suffered a nervous breakdown. The sketch opens with Sergeant X remembering the days preceding the Normandy invasion when a young girl, Esmé, had provided him with a moment of relief to offset the tedium and pressure of preinvasion camp life. Several weeks after the battle, the scene shifts to a civilian home where the sergeant is quartered with other soldiers. As he continues to tell the story, Sergeant X changes to a third-person narrator, a "disguise" rendered "so cunningly that even the cleverest reader will fail to recognize me," he believes. He is suffering from a breakdown, feeling his "mind dislodge itself and teeter, like insecure luggage on an overhead rack," when he looks at his mail and discovers a package that contains a letter from Esmé and her father's watch. Set against the boorish actions of his fellow soldiers and his own spiritually barren and dehumanized state, the letter and watch have the effect of bringing X out of his doldrums "with all his fac—with all his f-a-c-u-l-t-i-e-s intact."

The remaining stories reveal similar people who struggle to reconstruct their lives. "De Daumier-Smith's Blue Period" and "The Laughing Man," both told from a first-person point of view, are stories of young men searching for an identity as they look backward to experiences that had great impact on their lives. The opening story, "A Perfect Day for Bananafish," introduces Seymour Glass, a young man who with other members of his family later appears in *Franny and Zooey* (1961) and *Raise High the Roof Beam, Carpenters and Seymour, An Introduction* (1963). Like Holden Caulfield and Sergeant X, Glass is a typical Salinger character who seeks a resolution to his social maladjustment.

This exploration of the constant search for self was Salinger's major thematic contribution to the short story in the 1950s. In a period when the impact of war and the changing lifestyles of Americans became favorite topics for the short story, Salinger met the challenge and created a fictional world in which patterns of withdrawal and return were prominent. He, and therefore his characters, saw the American scene as a wasteland where only through continual striving and work could the individual maintain himself and survive. His characters' successes were usually small and the process of achieving them painful, but in approaching life slowly and sensibly they were able to transform their suffering into some kind of affirmation.

•   •   •

The stories of Irwin Shaw (1913—   ) deal chiefly with what people thought and did during the war years and the decade that followed. Although his works do not emphasize the psychological effects of the postwar years with as much clarity as do Salinger's, they portray a range of character types who try to come to grips with problems that seem particularly alarming in modern society. His first two collections, *Sailor Off the Bremen and Other Stories* (1939) and *Welcome to the City and Other Stories* (1942) were followed by *Act of Faith and Other Stories* (1946). *Mixed Company: Collected Short Stories* (1950) contains thirty-seven works selected from earlier editions.

The first story of *Mixed Company,* the often-anthologized "The Girls in Their Summer Dresses," is a good example of a Shaw tale that concentrates on a contemporary problem: the failure of marriage when each partner sees the other as mere convenience. Written in a lighter vein than is typical of Shaw, this story illustrates his tendency to overdramatize. Many of his stories are very effective, especially those concerned with war, but too often his situations are melodramatic. The reader is easily able to discern the "good guys" from the "bad guys," and the resolution of conflicts tends to be clever. "Sailor off the Bremen" is just such a work. Although it contains a good deal of suspense, the action occurs so rapidly and is the product of so many diverse ideologies that by story's end the reader is confused. In addition, Shaw's characters are too often identifiable as types. In "Sailor," Charlie is the agent of justice, Ernest the innocent victim, Lueger the personification of evil. The story may emphasize that the desire for revenge is sometimes justifiable, but Shaw's didactic tone makes the climax almost trivial.

"Act of Faith" is better, if only because it is more moving and convincing in its treatment of racial problems in the context of war. Shaw investigates similar issues in some of his other war stories: "Gunner's Passage," probably the best of these works; "Hamlets of the World"; "The City Was in Total Darkness"; "The Priest"; "Medal from Jerusalem"; "The Man with One Arm," to name a few. In light of the war as a major event in twentieth-century life, Shaw does present a vivid picture of the impact it had on its participants.

•   •   •

Equally intriguing vignettes of the effects of war on the decade are offered in the short stories of Robert Lowry (1919—   ). If only through sheer volume,

Lowry's stories of the Second World War are impressive. The best and first of these collections is *The Wolf That Fed Us* (1949). Whether Lowry is describing men in action, as in "The Wolf That Fed Us," or the effects that military service and war have had on its observers, as in the story of the wife who must resolve for herself the implications of her husband's impending overseas duty ("Layover in El Paso"), Lowry effectively reveals the feelings and actions of characters set in a specific time and place. The boundaries of Lowry's fictional world expand in later volumes—*Happy New Year, Kamerades!* (1954), *The Last Party* (1956), *New York Call Girl* (1958), and *Party of Dreamers* (1962)—but his best stories are those that deal with war.

·   ·   ·

Kay Boyle (1903—   ), too, deals with the impact of war on people. In fact, war and political confrontation provide the bulk of material for her fiction. However, as an early contributor to *The New Yorker,* she published several collections before the war: *Wedding Day and Other Stories* (1930), *First Lover and Other Stories* (1933), and *The White Horses of Vienna and Other Stories* (1936). The best of these prewar sketches were collected in *Thirty Stories* (1946). As a commentator on manners, Boyle has depicted the universal themes of love, marriage, and death. Like Henry James, she spent much of her life abroad so that many of her stories have an international flavor.

"Winter Night" depicts the relationships among a mother, her daughter, and a babysitter, and reveals Boyle's concern with the way in which events can be disrupted by war. In another story from the collection, "Effigy of War," originally appearing in a 1940 issue of *The New Yorker,* Boyle shows the destructive impact war has had on civilians at a seaside resort. Her vision is satiric as she treats two types of victims. The first is an individual who is not officially a part of the "war effort," the second, "the national of an alien country." The leader of the mob who assaults the civilians is ironically portrayed as a likely leader in wartime—the man who vehemently asserts his nationalism. As the story reaches its climax, the man and his mob attack a group of "foreigners" and use their flag with "religious fervor" as a symbol of their nationalism and as an excuse for their actions. Although the story is set in France at the beginning of the Second World War, it is not specifically about that war. Boyle's observations are intended to be universal, as she shows how people are swayed by the tensions and spirit of conflict.

In Boyle's later collection, *The Smoking Mountain: Stories of Germany During the Occupation* (1951), she again demonstrates her understanding of people and their motives by dealing with the aftermath of war. Set in the American zone in postwar Germany, these stories reveal that while winners and losers can superficially adjust to their roles, they can never relate to each other.

• • •

Exploring another group affected by the events and manners of postwar America is Elizabeth Enright (1909—1968). Three collections of stories reflect her interest in the world of children. Her first volume, *Borrowed Summer and Other Stories* (1946), was followed by *The Moment Before the Rain* (1955) and *The Riddle of the Fly and Other Stories* (1959). In "The Playground," from her second collection, Enright describes a day in the life of Nina Bernson, a young girl who encounters the real world with her friends. As she and her friends discuss their mothers' divorces in a matter-of-fact way, three events interrupt their fun. First, they see a couple making love; then they are chased by a potential child molester; and finally, they must save one of their group from drowning. Yet as much as these events have probably wounded them psychologically, Nina's response to her mother's question, "What did you do?" is, "Oh, nothing. . . . Swam. Played. Nothing much." Enright's ability to capture the mind of a child is unerring in this and other stories.

Enright also treats "rebellion in old age," as in "The Moment Before the Rain." Here, Mrs. Dacey and Mr. Kendall discuss the impending marriage of their grandchildren and acknowledge the desolation of old age. Told from Mrs. Dacey's viewpoint, the story reveals the personal anguish of the two as they recognize what age has taken away from them. In "The House by the River," the opening story in *The Riddle of the Fly,* Enright shows the effect on a young boy of hearing from an old woman about the death of her husband. These stories underscore Enright's sensitive appraisal of people and the triumphs and tragedies of their daily existence.

• • •

Mark Van Doren (1874—1972) also writes about childhood or the remembrances of childhood in *The Witch of Ramoth and Other Tales* (1950), *Short Stories of Mark Van Doren* (1950), *Nobody Said a Word and Other Stories* (1953), *Home with Hazel and Other Stories* (1957), and *Collected Stories* (1962).

In the last collection, Van Doren reveals the special qualities of children's imaginations and points up the differences between youth and age. "The Witch of Ramoth" is a tale of the supernatural written for children. Two siblings are frightened by an old woman who they come to realize has supernatural powers. They cannot find their home and soon discover that no one can see or hear them. The ending is equally mysterious as the children appear to be under the witch's spell. "A Wild West Place" contrasts the attitudes between a grandmother and granddaughter; "Grandison and Son" examines alienation between father and son; "Abide with Me" highlights the reconciliation between mother and son. Whether the main characters are children or adults trying to resolve the crises of life by examining the past or looking forward to the future, they are excellent examples of people caught in problems of their own making.

• • •

Like Van Doren, Wallace Stegner (1909—   ) presents the conflict between generations and the ensuing complications in *The Women on the Wall* (1950) and *The City of the Living* (1956). "Chip off the Old Block," from the first collection, is partly autobiographical and is typical of Stegner's ability to comment on the problems that arise when a twelve-year-old Montana boy is made "the man of the house" after his father is struck down with the flu. The boy's decisions, not always prudent, and his bravery in the face of danger, highlight his initiation into manhood. Similar themes surface in the other seventeen tales in this volume and in the eight stories of *The City of the Living*.

"The Blue-Winged Teal," for instance, reveals tension and conflict between a father and son in their attempts at reconciliation after the death of the boy's mother. Henry Lederer has had to quit college to take care of his father, whom he hates. He makes the older man a peace offering of nine blue-winged teals. It is not enough, however; the gift can neither salvage the present nor recapture the past. When he decides there will be no change in the relationship, Henry leaves "with the feeling he might have had in letting go of the hand of a friend too weak and too exhausted to cling any longer to their inadequate shared driftwood in a wide cold sea."

• • •

More prolific than Stegner, Warren Beck explores a wide variety of subjects in his four collections: *The Blue Sash, and Other Stories* (1940), *The First Fish, and Other Stories* (1947), *The Far Whistle, and Other Stories* (1951), and *The Rest Is Silence, and Other Stories* (1963). Beck concentrates on satiric depiction of the responsibilities men and women must face to offset prejudice, violence, and misunderstanding in the postwar years.

• • •

The stories of Charles Jackson (1903—1968) and William Goyen (1915—   ) explore these same themes. In two volumes published in the early 1950s, *The Sunnier Side: Twelve Arcadian Tales* (1950) and *Earthly Creatures: Ten Stories* (1953), Jackson uncovers the illusions of youth and shows how people destroy themselves when these illusions are shattered. Goyen's *Ghost and Flesh: Stories and Tales*

(1952) emphasizes the conflict between youth and age. His people seek ways of freeing themselves from the ghosts of the past so that they can understand the meaning of the present. Ironically, their attempts are often self-destructive.

• • •

While this group of authors was at work delineating American manners, others were writing about changes taking place in the South. Nowhere in the geography of American letters in the last thirty-five years has more fresh and original fiction surfaced than in the South, where writers have created a body of work that is the equal of any written in the postwar era. Following the example of William Faulkner, and inspired by the fragmented social landscape of a region that was still steeped in the traditions of the past, they portrayed the rural, and hence largely conservative, manners of a new generation of Southerners. Unlike their Northern counterparts, Southern stories of the decade tend to be tragic, rich in legend and myth, often populated by grotesque characters, and softened by the cadences of Southern speech. Of this new wave of short-story writers, few are the equal of Peter Taylor.

Although Taylor's stories detail the urban, middle-class world of his native Tennessee, they also mirror many of the tensions and complications that give shape and substance to the genre as it applies to all of contemporary America. Like his fellow storytellers, Taylor (1917—   ) focuses on a world torn by its reverence for traditions of the past and its necessary adherence to pretensions of the present. No longer able to survive through an allegiance to old-fashioned notions, no longer able to order their lives according to old loyalties, Taylor's people find themselves caught up in a world where blacks seek their freedom, women assert their independence, and children express their unwillingness to be seen and not heard. These new values that his Southerners are hesitant to accept are responsible for the disintegration of family structure and social order. Taylor's first two collections of stories, *A Long Fourth and Other Stories* (1948) and *The Widows of Thornton* (1954), reflect these changes.

All seven stories of *A Long Fourth* reveal a growing urban, industrial South. The title story is characteristic of the collection and brilliantly explores this changing world. Harriet Wilson, "just past fifty," her ineffectual doctor-husband "Sweetheart," their two tipsy daughters, Helena and Kate, and their son, together with Mattie and BT, the Negro servants, make up the household. The story tells the events surrounding the son's return to Nashville for a long weekend before he enters the army. The family crises that take place during this time are explosive, and they reflect the not-so-engaging side of Southern manners.

Taylor achieves his vivid portrait by concentrating on Harriet. As the story opens, she has to handle a number of emergencies. Mattie's son BT threatens to move away from Nashville to work in a factory, a move that upsets Mattie and turns the household upside down. Matters are not helped by the two daughters whose drunken behavior threatens plans for the weekend. Then Son arrives and brings with him a New York girl, whose ideas seem radical to the Wilsons and who seems to have too much influence on Son. Instead of a genteel weekend, complete with appropriate social amenities, the "long Fourth" becomes a forum for the discussion of inflammatory social and political ideas. The argument, for example, over the place of Negroes (Kate believes that "Southern white people have a great responsibility" toward blacks; Son counters with his newly formed idea that the people in the South "cannot expect to progress with the rest of the nation until they've forgotten their color line") is symptomatic of the changes that are taking place, and no one in Taylor's stories is immune from their effects. The portrait of the Wilson household vividly reveals the turmoil between the old and new South.

Because Taylor's South is uncertain of itself, it becomes a place where old values are fair game for skeptics and spokesmen for radical ideas. "A Spinster's Tale" and "The Fancy Woman" are especially good examples of these personal and social conflicts. Like "A Long Fourth," these are stories about women who appear to react most strongly to and are most affected by the changes in their society. Josie of "The Fancy Woman" and Elizabeth of "A Spinster's Tale" are, like Harriet, women whose ambivalence and wonder at these shifts in values give Taylor's stories their depth. Their inability to resolve conflicts and their ambiguous relationships with men are typical of Taylor's keen insight. Taylor suggests that women more than men are sensitive to the ironies of life that affect them profoundly.

In Taylor's next collection, *The Widows of Thornton,* the best-drawn characters are again women. In the opening story, perhaps the most compelling and skillful of the collection, Taylor continues to address the issues of old and new, tradition and innovation, order and change, past and present. "Their Losses" introduces three women, two of whom are spinsters and the third a married woman. Returning to Thornton with her aunt after a holiday, Miss Patty Bean decries the fading away of the old South—its values, its farmland, its towns—to her two traveling companions and former classmates, Ellen Louise Watkins and Cornelia Weatherby Warner. At breakfast, all three discuss the bleak landscape, the end of the old South, and death. Cornelia doesn't believe in mourning. For Miss Patty, this is sacrilege, as she feels mourning is an obligation, part of a tradition that represents a "prosperous and civilized existence," and taking her aunt to Memphis is therefore an act quite noble and natural. Ellen Watkins, the third member of the party who is bringing home the body of her mother for burial, falls somewhere between the conservative Patty and the liberal Cornelia in her allegiance to past values. Despite their differences, these women have one thing in common: all reflect a sense of melancholia for their unfulfilled lives. Their reunion on the train is neither beneficial nor pleasant. Like the other people in Taylor's stories, they are alone in an alien and unfriendly world.

The other characters in *The Widows of Thornton* are also affected by change. In "Cookie," for instance, Taylor portrays a wife comfortably settled in middle-aged stasis with a husband who no longer finds their relationship (chiefly characterized by a stiff, formal evening meal) either stimulating or rewarding. He comes home, eats his dinner, engages in what becomes a tedious and routine conversation, and then escapes. At the end of the story, Taylor uses the husband's car to suggest his disenchantment with the studied world of his wife and their servant, Cookie: "He began walking with light, sure steps, over the grass—their ugly, old voices. In the driveway, his car, bright and new and luxurious, was waiting for him." For the husband, his marriage is not bright, new, or luxurious.

In "A Wife of Nashville," the characters find it more difficult to escape the past. The Lovell household, for years beset by a series of servants who leave them for one reason or another, is faced, after long devoted service, with the loss of Jess McGhee, the very best of the lot. Taylor constructs the story using a series of flashbacks, each of which describes the virtues and idiosyncrasies of the departed servants, to concentrate on his major theme: the loneliness and isolation that affect both blacks and whites in the new South. He establishes with great poignancy the special kinship that develops over the years between Helen Ruth Lovell and Jess. At the end of the story, when the men of the Lovell family are shocked at the inexplicable departure of Jess, Helen Ruth alone understands.

"A Wife of Nashville" is an excellent example of how Taylor's style creates interest and meaning. Robert Penn Warren describes Taylor's method of storytelling in his introduction to *A Long Fourth*. He states that it is a "natural style, one based in conversation and the family tale, with the echo of the spoken word, with the texture of some narrator's mind." Warren's evaluation suggests that unlike some Southern and Northern contemporaries, Taylor finds his subjects in the quieter, though no less tragic, dramas of domestic situations and family affairs. Because of his style, vivid character portrayal, and command of form, Taylor is one of the masters of the contemporary story of manners. His representation of middle-class values and standards of conduct exposes their hollowness in an ironic and significant way.

•   •   •

Even more compelling than Taylor's study of the effects of the changing American scene are the stories of Eudora Welty (1909—   ). Welty combines elements of comedy, pathos, myth, horror, and fantasy to reveal the conflict in a character's ability to distinguish appearance and reality, a sense of the past and perception of the present, and obligations to the social world and to self. Like Taylor's *The Widows of Thornton,* Welty's *The Golden Apples* (1949) describes the lives of various family members in her fictional Morgana, Mississippi. Perhaps not as effective as her two earlier collections, *A Curtain of Green* (1941) and *The Wide Net* (1943), *The Golden Apples* nonetheless illustrates Welty's methods of storytelling.

In "Shower of Gold," the first story in the collection, Welty introduces the history of King MacLain, one of the most compelling characters in her fiction. A traveling salesman who also fancies himself a great lover, he is presented as a figure of Southern lore whose exploits are both mysterious and legendary. Cast as a comic version of Jove, MacLain also appears in two other stories, "Sir Rabbit" and "The Wanderers," the latter describing his homecoming after years of roving. King's two sons, Randall and Eugene, appear in "The Whole World Knows," a soliloquy by Randall dealing with the effects of his wife Jinny's infidelity, and in "Miser from Spain," a story about Eugene's life in San Francisco. The other stories in the collection recount the lives of other Morgana citizens, but the MacLain sketches are the best.

The Golden Apples is unified by Welty's use of the mythical quest for the golden apples. Just as King MacLain is a wanderer searching for gold of his own, so, too, are other residents searching for meaning in their lives. Some may leave Morgana for a time, but eventually all return in an attempt to understand their ties with the town. Even more important than Welty's sense of place in these stories (most of them take place in Mississippi) is her emphasis on individual identity. She is interested in probing the enigma of people caught in traps created by their inability to solve life's mysteries. The events in her stories are simple, but the people and their responses to these events are complex.

In her fourth collection, *The Bride of the Innisfallen and Other Stories* (1955), three stories take place in the contemporary South, another is set in the Civil War era, and two more are based on her European experiences; the final story takes place on a mythical island in the Mediterranean. While her four Southern pieces—"Ladies in Spring," "Ken," "No Place for You, My Love," and "The Burning"—are quite in the Welty tradition of revealing her characters' limitations, mortality, and cosmos, the other three are not as effective. Even though they appear to lack the force of her earlier work, they are successful because Welty brings to them the same unerring quality she brings to all her stories: she is a master of analyzing the human condition, whether the people live in rural Mississippi or in Cork, Ireland, the setting of "The Bride of the Innisfallen."

In this story, the bride, a girl who has been lost in the frustration of an unsuccessful marriage in England, comes to realize the possibilities of a new life as she walks about the streets of Cork seeing vegetation flowering and children in confirmation dresses running up and down the street.

The key to Welty's success and skills lies in her willingness to take chances. In an essay, "How I Write," she explains that often the "most exacting and sometimes the simplest appearing work is brought off (when it does not fail) on the sharp edge of experiment, not in dim, reneging safety." Regardless of place and time, Welty's stories of dying husbands, cosmetic saleswomen, aging men, and simple field hands, blacks and whites, Southerners and Northerners, work because of her amazing diversity of subject, style, and technique.

• • •

Of Eudora Welty's contemporaries who also liked to take chances, certainly Flannery O'Connor (1925—1964) is the most fascinating. Like Welty, she uses the South as her province, but her characters are more grotesque than Welty's. They are a collection of misfits and pariahs, characters who assume abnormal and bizarre attitudes toward each other and themselves. Her first and best collection is *A Good Man Is Hard to Find and Other Stories* (1955). In these ten stories, O'Connor blends comedy and tragedy in her depiction of people whose problems are not caused solely by their social or family upbringing, but by a basic flaw in their characters. "Good Country People," for instance, portrays people's physical and mental infirmities. Everyone in the tale suffers from some degrading, crippling condition that distorts and demeans their human dignity. Hulga's maimed body is symbolic of her maimed soul. Because she has an artificial leg, she has changed her life to reflect the change in her body. She has a doctoral degree in philosophy, has announced herself an atheist, and has changed her legal name from Joy to Hulga. When she meets a Bible salesman who proclaims himself to be a "country boy," Hulga decides to seduce him. In their rendezvous in the barn loft, Hulga's assumed superiority is revealed to be spurious. Not only is the salesman a false Christian—as he disappears down the hayloft ladder with her artificial leg, he shouts to her that he has "believed in nothing" ever since he was born—he has turned out to be more than her match. O'Connor reveals Hulga's pride and intellectual posturing to be only gullibility and ignorance.

The conclusion to "Good Country People" illustrates O'Connor's method of composition. Because she records the events in her stories in such a casual manner, the reader is lulled into believing that little is happening. This flow, however, is characteristically broken by an explosive ending, delivered with such ironic impact that it forms a startling climax to O'Connor's portrayal of distortions in modern life.

Distortions are also the subject of "The Artificial Nigger," a story about the estrangement and reconciliation of two Georgians, an old man named Mr. Head and his grandson Nelson, who go to the city for a visit. Nelson has never seen a black man, and the opening pages show his first encounter with one. He expresses awe for a huge Negro man wearing a ruby stickpin and an unexpected affection for an enormous black woman. His response is contrasted with an incident in which he knocks down a white woman carrying groceries. The grandfather in a moment of shame denies his grandson's existence when he says, "This is not my boy . . . I never seen him before." This causes a rift between the two, and O'Connor's reconciliation comes when they see a plaster statue of a Negro (eating watermelon) who is supposed to represent God's grace: "They could both feel it dissolving their differences like an action of mercy." Both exclaim, "An artificial nigger." This communication transforms them, as Mr. Head is described as an "ancient child" and Nelson as a "miniature old man." The dramatic ending is a surprise, and it achieves the effect of shocking both the characters and the reader into an awareness of their infirmities.

The remainder of the stories are not as effective, for they fail to create a balance between O'Connor's grotesque vision and her imaginative power. They reveal her too frequent tendency to end a story with death. "The Baptism" concludes with a drowning, "A Late Encounter with the Enemy" with a corpse, and the title story, "A Good Man Is Hard to Find," with the murder of an entire family. Such gratuitous violence is a reflection of her tendency to deal in extremes.

• • •

Another Southern woman writer uses the grotesque even more boldly than Flannery O'Connor. Carson McCullers (1917—1967) in her collection, *The Ballad of the Sad Cafe* (1951), presents a cast of characters who are failures and outcasts in a world in which traditional values are no longer visible. Three of the selections in the book are novellas *(The Heart Is a Lonely Hunter, Reflections in a Golden Eye,* and *The Member of the Wedding); each* is a brilliant, longer version of the perversities McCullers presents in the short stories, reflecting the themes of loneliness, alienation, and frustrations of love that have become her trademark.

"The Ballad of the Sad Cafe" best illustrates her technique. Here McCullers creates a gruesome trio of caricatures. Amelia, a six-foot bootlegger, lives in a decrepit shack with two men who are equal to those in any horror story: Macy, her husband who supposedly carries in his pocket the severed ear of a man he once killed in a fight; and Lyman, a sinister-looking four-foot dwarf. This threesome forms an unusual "family" whose adventures reveal their almost inhuman behavior and make-up. Despite such features as a macabre love triangle, a bone-cracking wrestling match between Amelia and Macy, and a violent ending, McCullers avoids turning the story into a gruesome melodrama by injecting folk humor from time to time. Throughout, she uses ballad motifs to humanize her characters and to make their behavior less morbid.

When Lyman the dwarf arrives at Amelia's house, she takes him in, offers him food and drink, and sets up a relationship, that although strange, begins to transform both of them into more likeable human beings. Eventually Amelia's house becomes a cafe to which customers come to escape their melancholy. This lasts only six years, however, just until Macy arrives. Years before, Amelia and Macy had been married for ten stormy days, and with his reappearance the story moves toward what the town sees as an inevitable battle. The description of this final match of two "epic" combatants is presented with a combination of humor and realism. At the end, when Lyman, the appointed referee, announces Macy the winner, the two men break up Amelia's possessions, exit town together, and leave the woman a recluse.

McCullers's use of ballad motifs (dreams, superstitions, music) creates an atmosphere that makes the tale mirror the rituals of romance. By turning the story and its characters into something almost allegorical, McCullers comments on the choices inherent in every lover's affairs. She suggests that passion is the dominant element in human relationships, and that to be both the lover and the beloved is part of the ideal every human being seeks. Even though that love is distorted, there is no reason for it not to exist in the lives of misfits and outcasts. To transcend spiritual isolation in love, then, becomes her most haunting theme.

• • •

Another of the writers belonging to the Southern renaissance, Truman Capote (1924—   ) achieved his fame in the 1960s and 1970s, but was recognized as an important writer in the early 1950s. His early stories, collected in *A Tree of Night and Other Stories* (1951), reveal his talent for short fiction. Capote not only emphasizes the decadent and macabre aspects of Southern gothic fiction, but reveals his ability to treat such major modern themes as loneliness, the search for individual identity, and alienation. In "Jug of Silver," for instance, he blends psychological realism with comic vision to tell the story of a search for the pot at the end of the rainbow. Narrated by a small-town observer, the story introduces Appleseed, a twelve-year-old boy (thought by some to be eight) who guesses the correct amount of nickels and dimes in a jug. This "jug of silver," a gimmick thought up by Ed Marshall, the Valhall druggist, becomes the object of controversy by story's end. Young Appleseed, a stranger who appears in the town with his sister, is said to have psychic powers because he was "born with a caul" on his head. When he correctly guesses the amount in the jar (to the very nickel), the townspeople cry foul, but are never able to solve the mystery of how he did it. This mystery becomes a legend that is retold by Marshall every Christmas day to the Baptist Bible class.

Capote's fictional world, peopled by vivid characters, the events of which are told from the point of view of a town representative, is a key element in his stories. There are actually two worlds portrayed in "Jug of Silver" and many of his other stories: one, a realistic and humorous daytime world, the other a nocturnal place often characterized by its illusory nature. Capote's characters fade in and out of the action thereby providing the stories with an eerie quality much like those tales of his fellow Southerners. The humorous touch of Appleseed's sister, for instance, joyously announcing that the money her brother won will be used to buy her a new set of white false teeth, is offset by Appleseed's mysterious powers and the pair's eventual disappearance.

This atmosphere is also found in "Miriam," another of his stories of children. A middle-aged woman, Mrs. Miller, is frightened by her meeting with a strange child. Mrs. Miller moves throughout the story as through a dream. Objects lose shape, strange sounds emanate from rooms in her apartment, and she becomes increasingly terrified by Miriam's appearances and disappearances. In this story, as in "The Headless Hawk," "Master Misery," and "Shut a Final Door," Capote elucidates in a much more vivid manner than in "Jug of Silver," the contrasts between illusion and reality, the forces of good and evil, light and dark. The people in these stories, whether adults or children, are obsessed by their fear of the unknown.

"A Tree of Night" is an especially good example of Capote's dreamlike world. Unlike other gothic writers, he uses gothicism to evoke a sense of evil rather than to provide psychological portraits of characters. This story is disturbing because it presents so many possible answers to the questions it asks. Kay, the main character, is a college student riding alone on the train back to college after her uncle's funeral. The tension surfaces when she meets a weird couple who pay an undesired amount of attention to her. As if through a sense of déjà vu, Kay thinks she recognizes them, but is terrified by the thought. When the man leans over and touches her cheek for no apparent reason, the contact between them is established. As the story rapidly reaches its conclusion, Kay is slowly mesmerized and at the end, as they take her purse and draw her raincoat over her head, the reader is stunned. Capote's dreamlike atmosphere has a psychological effect on the action as it draws the reader into a surrealistic world of dreams and the supernatural. The effect is both compelling and unsettling.

Capote's second collection, *Breakfast at Tiffany's: A Short Novel and Three Stories* (1958), however, is quite different in tone and effect. Of the short stories, "A Christmas Memory" (the other two are "House of Flowers" and "A Diamond Guitar") is considered one of Capote's best. A seven-year-old tells the story of a young man and his "sixty-something" cousin. As best friends whose battles with relatives are portrayed as comic impediments to their goal of gathering the ingredients for baking Christmas fruitcakes, the two provide a lighthearted look at the last Christmas they spend together. The mirthful quality of this story is quite different from the somber tone of Capote's other works.

• • •

The four collections of short stories by Tennessee Williams (1914—   ) reveal worlds very similar to those of Capote and O'Connor. His characters resemble those in his plays. In fact, many of the stories were early versions of the ideas he later used in works for the stage: "Portrait of a Girl in Glass" for *The Glass Menagerie;* "Three Players of a Summer Game" for *Cat on a Hot Tin Roof;* "Man Bring Up This Road" for *The Milk Train Doesn't Stop Here Anymore;* and "The Night of the Iguana" for the play of the same name. In all of his work, Williams portrays both adolescents and adults who are disillusioned and frustrated. They are men and women who are different, and because of their eccentricities have a need to see the world clearly. They succeed, but end up recognizing the horror that is present. As characters lost in time, they tend not to belong to their own world or to any other. Like his Southern contemporaries, Williams's stories become portraits of a generation that views itself as displaced.

One Arm and Other Stories (1948) is Williams's first collection. "Portrait of a Girl in Glass" exemplifies the people in his fictional world. Laura is a girl who "made no positive motion toward the world but stood at the edge of the water so to speak, with feet that anticipated too much cold to move." She needs to be "shoved . . . roughly forward" to overcome her fear of the world. As the story comes to a climax, she never does. Similar tales of meandering in and out of life make up the major stories in *One Arm.* In "The Field of Blue Children," two loners briefly meet, love, and drift away from each other into their own world; in the title story, a young man finds himself penned "in a corner and only waiting for death"; in "The Malediction," Lucio finds a cat, Nitchevo, wounded and dying. He sees in the cat's eyes a reflection of his own life: "They were full to the amber brims with all the secrets and sorrows the world can answer our ceaseless questioning with loneliness—yes. Hunger. Bewilderment. Pain. They wanted no more."

In *Hard Candy: A Book of Stories* (1954), Williams's second collection, similar themes and techniques appear. Throughout, the individual's confrontation with a truth too painful to bear is the highlight of the action. In "Three Players of a Summer Game," Brick Pollitt, former athlete and current alcoholic, is driven by his wife Margaret to a condition that turns him into a wreck of a man. Margaret controls Brick: "It was as though she had her lips fastened to some invisible wound in his body through which drained out of him and flowed into her the assurance and vitality that he had owned before marriage." By the end of the story, Brick has given in to Margaret's hammerlock on his life and is "no longer a human, but a babbling and goggling wreck." He has become her "boy" and she his conqueror. Other stories reveal the same emphasis on the unlived life that is not worth living. In "The Vine," "The Important Thing," "The Resemblance Between a Violin Case and a Coffin," and "The Mattress by the Tomato Patch," Williams's protagonists are all afflicted by their loss of innocence and inability to face reality.

By the time his third collection, *The Knightly Quest: A Novella and Some Short Stories* (1961), was published, Williams's craft had diminished. His best fiction by this time had already been written, his best plays already produced. *The Knightly Quest,* the novella, is a strange story of Gewinner Pearce, who returns home after years of travel to discover that great changes have taken place. The Project, a top-secret government plan, obsesses the town, and the Laughing-Boy Drive-In has been built directly across from the Pearce family mansion, having been given a ninety-nine-year lease by Gewinner's brother. The story is almost farcical as it follows the antics of Gewinner and the townspeople responding to these changes. Gewinner, for instance, is launched into space on a knightly quest, a part of the story made unbelievable by Williams's treatment of the entire incident. The other stories are more vintage Williams as they explore earlier themes.

It is clear that Williams's reputation as a major American literary figure rests in his dramatic achievements. Yet the early stories are important, too, especially as the best of them mirror the themes of his most remarkable plays, for they establish his place in the Southern renaissance.

• • •

With the stories of Robert Penn Warren (1905—   ) in *The Circus in the Attic* (1948), the theme of individual dignity is again dominant. Warren was born a Southerner, and has remained one spiritually, but his allegiance has been complex. Perhaps because of the diversity of his experiences with academic and nonacademic people, Northerners and Southerners, intellectuals and laborers, his stories tend to comment not only on regional values, but on universal ones as well. Like the work of his best counterparts, his tales become more than local color; they mirror the manners of an era in America.

Most of his short fiction is a painful celebration of young men's first steps into the real world. Perhaps the most outstanding is "Blackberry Winter." Here a man in his early forties recalls his initiation into manhood. As a boy, he had been attracted to a stranger who had come to work on his family's farm during a period of torrential rains and severe flooding. When the man left the farm because of an argument, the boy went with him vicariously. At the end of the story, the narrator, remembering the incident with chagrin, realizes he never could accept the devastation and the poverty of his youth, and thus tried to escape that world and its responsibility by not being an active part of it. In telling the story from the point of view of a man looking back in time to his youth, Warren accents the effect of change, not just on the young man in particular, but also on the South and young men in general. The narrator has been overcome with guilt, everpresent in Warren's stories, and he is not sure how to respond to it after so many years.

"When the Light Gets Green" also illustrates Warren's thematic and narrative techniques. Once again the story is told from the viewpoint of an adult looking back to his childhood. The speaker wants to discuss his relations with his grandfather as they were when they existed, and not reveal what he has thought about them as an adult. To accomplish this, Warren has his narrator show what he understood during the actual time of the relationship without comment from his present self. This technique discloses that the boy was mature enough to understand his feelings, but too immature to comprehend what they meant for either his grandfather or himself. This technique has the advantage of telling the story from a series of random recollections, rather than having to include details that are not germane to the effect Warren wants to achieve. The boy recollects only those incidents that had meaning for him in his youth. Warren therefore provides the reader with a sense of sharing and understanding life, instead of merely giving information. Like Warren's other initiation stories, this style enables him to emphasize the young man's guilt. The grandfather had waited years for love, but the grandson cannot love. As an adult, he feels guilty about his inability to comprehend this deficiency.

The other stories in *The Circus in the Attic* contain similar recognition scenes. In "Christmas Gift," "Testament of Flood," and "Her Own People," Warren shows characters who create guilt as a response to their sense of imprisonment. Like the misinformed Jack Burden of *All the King's Men,* Warren's major novel of the period, his characters search for an identity in the present only to discover that they cannot escape their past.

• • •

The short stories of Caroline Gordon (1895—1981) also celebrate the stability to be found in the past. Like Warren, she stresses the need for individual responsibility in coming to grips with the social disintegration of the modern North and South. Specifically, her stories reveal the contrast between the agrarian society whose values reflect the hierarchy of the early South, and the urban society in which skepticism and impersonal relationships are characteristic of the industrial age.

As a disciple of Henry James and believer in his theory of psychological realism, Gordon concentrates on the conduct of people in their relationships with others and the changes that must and do take place in these relationships. For Gordon, the need to reveal the subtle shifts in people's attitudes toward each other, and to do so in a way that describes their emotions, is of prime importance. Gordon also realizes that James's use of a restricted third-person point of view is the most effective technique. By filtering the events of the story through a single narrator, she can disclose the feelings of the narrator toward himself, others, and his place in the world. This information is not always reliable, but it does serve to enhance form and spiritual authority in her work.

Almost any of the stories in *The Forest of the South* (1945), her first collection, illustrate her use of point of view. "Old Red," one of the stories in which Gordon uses Aleck Murray as the central consciousness, is the tale of a man who values his freedom above all else. We understand his limited view of other characters and come to know his thoughts on everything: his food, his family, the nature of time. As these thoughts are filtered through the character, Gordon's themes surface. First, the reader learns that fishing is Aleck's life; it is an obsession, a passion, in many ways an art for him. He fishes not as a hobby, but as a way of finding himself. Also, for him, time is the measure of a man's life. Everyone else in the story is afraid of time, and according to Aleck, wastes it. His son-in-law Stephen is for Aleck a "Poor boy, dead to the world," who leads a disordered, abstract life. Ironically, as the story progresses, it is Aleck who realizes, "It was he, not Steve, that was the queer one!"

Throughout the action, Aleck is aware that he is fighting a battle against those who disapprove of his philosophy of life. The central moment comes when Aleck remembers "Old Red," the wily fox that eluded capture because of his ability to escape every hunter's ploy. Aleck like the fox is a hunted figure. From Old Red he learns two lessons: first, that freedom is most important to him; and second, that like the fox hunt, his family's attempts at trapping him are sport. At the end of the story, he wins his race against time and the hunters.

Caroline Gordon's story is effective and provocative in several ways. Aleck Murray and his family symbolize the essential conflict between the individual and a society that tends to departmentalize life and make a man feel guilty over whatever freedom he can salvage. Gordon's narrative technique effectively allows her main character to define his basic values. She uses similar techniques and themes in the rest of the stories of *The Forest of the South*.

In "The Last Day in the Field," another Aleck Murray story, Gordon creates a vivid portrait of the character's philosophical cast of mind, his stoicism, and his nature, by revealing the internal conflicts between him and his fishing companion. These differences, when played out against the action, create the dramatic tension that ultimately reveals Aleck's failing health and his almost ritual farewell to the hunt.

Elsewhere in the volume, Gordon charts the disillusionment of her central characters. In "The Brilliant Leaves," love disintegrates into frustration when a young girl realizes an affair has changed with the passage of time; in "Her Quaint Honour," the narrator watches a barn full of tobacco spoil because the man in charge yields momentarily to his passion for the black wife of a hired hand; in "The Forest of the South," one of Gordon's Civil War stories, a girl is ruined by those who, like herself, fought for an ideal the consequences of which they were unable to foresee. In all of these stories, Gordon compares the grandeur of the early South and its diminished present with men and women whose past has also diminished over time.

As a regionalist, she stands with the best of her contemporary Southern writers, but her major contributions to the short story come from her portrayal of character. For the most part, her stories seem to have little plot, but on second glance they reveal the manners of the South in the middle of the twentieth century and the dynamic quality of human relationships between ordinary men and women.

• • •

Similar tales of Southerners undergoing the rigors of daily life are found in *The Black Prince and Other Stories* (1955) by Shirley Ann Grau (1929—   ) and in the first collection of stories by Doris Betts (1932—   ). Although neither has the range of Gordon, Betts is especially astute at revealing character. In "The Sympathetic Visitor," the opening tale from *The Gentle Insurrection and Other Stories* (1954), she describes the trauma of a white woman as she travels to a black household in Rabbittown to learn the details of a murder. Because "Niggers always left her feeling tired," a refrain sounded several times throughout the story, the traveler leaves Rabbittown, not with warmth or sympathy, but with "nameless horror" at what she has learned.

Like the best stories in the collection ("A Sense of Honor," "Mr. Shawn and Father Scott," "The Gentle Insurrection," "The Very Old Are Beautiful"), "The Sympathetic Visitor" reveals Betts's ability to write stories that exhibit a diversity of characters and reactions to everyday pressures. Whether the characters are young or old, black or white, girls having babies or old men facing death, she unmasks their personalities in a realistic and unsentimental fashion.

• • •

Jesse Stuart (1907—   ) also emphasizes the commonplace in his stories collected in *Tales from the Plum Grove Hills* (1946) and *Clearing in the Sky and Other Stories* (1950). Stuart sketches life in the hills of Kentucky and describes days in the lives of people who face trauma with an unyielding spirit. Unlike some of his Southern contemporaries, Stuart's characters are not grotesque, nor does he rely on the bizarre. His families are simple people who recall the past with affection (as in "Grandpa Birdwell's Last Battle" or "I Remember Molly"), the manners and superstitions of the countryside with humor ("Fitified Man," "Frog-Trouncin' Contest"), the place of nature in their lives ("Thanksgiving Hunter," "The Storm"), and death with respect ("Death Has Two Good Eyes"). Stuart is not on a par with Taylor, Welty, or Warren as a technician. He is primarily a local-color writer, yet his stories of hill people, told as though they were being shared with neighbors over the local crackerbarrel, have an intimacy and immediacy that is appealing.

· · ·

Although Southern writers produced most of the important short fiction in the postwar decade, others belonging to no distinct school were just as prolific and made significant contributions in their portraits of local manners. The best of them escaped the pitfalls of producing work that was a product of regional dialects, habits, and traditions only. Their sense of milieu enabled them to turn the regional into the archetypal, the specific into the universal.

The short stories of James T. Farrell reveal a vivid portrait of life in Chicago. Farrell (1904—1979) published four collections in the dozen years after 1945: *When Boyhood Dreams Come True* (1946), *The Life Adventurous and Other Stories* (1947), *French Girls Are Vicious and Other Stories* (1955), and *A Dangerous Woman and Other Stories* (1957). Although he is a prolific writer of novels, novellas, short stories, poems, and literary criticism, and although his cycles of novels starring Studs Lonigan, Danny O'Neill, and Bernard Carr have created a mythology of their own, he has never received much serious critical attention. For the most part, like John O'Hara, he is a photographic realist who presents a literal report of life as seen from the outside. He traces the personal destinies of his characters as they wander from one church parish to another, from one job to another, or from one woman to another.

Despite their lack of narrative variety, his short stories do achieve something that O'Hara's fail to accomplish. With his characters, many of whom are drawn from his novels and appear in story after story, Farrell creates a fictional world composed of types brought together by common problems. Like Chekhov, Farrell concentrates on character rather than action, and it is this emphasis that makes his stories vivid portrayals of urban manners.

· · ·

Also writing about life in the Midwest is Jessamyn West (1907—   ). Although she spent most of her life in California, her first collection, *The Friendly Persuasion* (1946), depicts the world of a Quaker family in Indiana. These fourteen stories of the Jess Birdwell family are sympathetic treatments of family problems. "Shivaree Before Breakfast" is interesting for its use of the initiation theme in which a young boy is shocked by his glimpse into the adult world. West's method of allowing the family boys to understand and respond to an unexpected discovery is well-handled. They begin by arranging a shivaree (wedding serenade) for Alf and Molly. When they realize the two are not married, they are shocked and find it hard to accept. West avoids the sentimental with a good bit of irony and turns what could have been a pathetic situation into a humorous one.

She continues her portrait of Quaker life in the other stories. Again, she uses irony to reveal the intricate customs and traditions of a religious group infrequently fictionalized. Her rendering of the rural atmosphere in this collection and in the later *Love, Death, and the Ladies' Drill Team* (1953) is effective.

• • •

Texas is the scene of many of William Humphrey's (1925—   ) stories. In *The Last Husband and Other Stories* (1953), Humphrey's concern is with small-town manners and mores. In a typical story, "Quail for Mr. Forester," a young boy reveals his family's experience when Mr. Forester, a member of an antebellum, aristocratic family who has gone into the hardware business in the postwar South, comes for dinner. Conversation is principally concerned with the decline of the old world and contrasts the values of the past with those of the present. At story's end, the boy, impressed deeply by Mr. Forester's tales, feels with his parents that "there is no hope for him in these mean times." The difference in social class portrayed through the boy's eyes is characteristic of the Texas Humphrey displays in *The Last Husband*. Lost in the glory of the past, his characters find little solace in their improved but unromantic place in the present.

• • •

The stories of William Saroyan (1908—1981) are filled with bursts of local color. In addition to plays and novels, Saroyan published eight volumes of short fiction. His first collection, *The Daring Young Man on the Flying Trapeze* (1934), introduces the major themes and articulates the style used in most of his later collections: *The Assyrian and Other Stories* (1950), *Love* (1955), *The Whole Voyald and Other Stories* (1956), *My Kind of Crazy Wonderful People* (1966), and *The Man with the Heart in the Highlands and Other Stories* (1968).

With the publication of *The Daring Young Man* at age twenty-five, Saroyan established his reputation as a serious writer. Although most of the stories are autobiographical and lack traditional plot, they do establish his philosophy of writing and reveal his background. Unlike other social realists writing in the 1930s, many of whom emphasized the dismal aspects of the period, Saroyan, while certainly evoking the setting and tone of the period, does so to highlight the people and their problems rather than to comment on the causes of the depression. With this emphasis on character and action, Saroyan deals effectively with loneliness, alienation, and the inability of people to achieve lasting relationships.

Later stories written after the Second World War are different in both tone and style, although they continue to be autobiographical. Characteristic of these collections are prefaces written to justify and sometimes to apologize for his writing.

• • •

James A. Michener (1907—   ) is recognized today more as the author of epic-length novels than of short stories. Yet his stories, collected in *Tales of the South Pacific* (1947) and *Return to Paradise* (1951), were his first ventures into fiction. Not a major innovator or technician in the short story tradition of the decade, Michener is important for his depiction of place, time, and mood. In these postwar years, his stories played to the romantic tastes of his readers. Rather than Farrell's seamy Chicago dives, O'Hara's New York streets, or Auchincloss's upper class mansions, Michener's exotic and faraway places appealed to an American audience seeking to escape the war years. Yet, ironically, Michener's stories are not always escape. Like the best writers since Henry James, Michener combines the elements of romance and realism to portray contemporary society. The settings may be romantic, but the action is always real. His war stories ("Coral Sea," "The Sea," "The Milk Run," "Alligator," among others) in *Tales of the South Pacific* are realistic in their portrayal of fighting and death. His other stories of the war years are equally vivid in their disclosure of men and women caught up in history.

• • •

America's love affair with Michener's tales of the South Seas was matched after the war by the rising popularity of a new genre: science fiction. Like those tales of romance that allowed people to live their daydreams and momentarily escape problems, pressures, and pollution, science fiction created a similar release. Published at a time when the advances of science were fashionable topics of conversation, these tales of fantasy stimulated interest, especially among the

young. Of the science fiction writers in the period, Ray Bradbury (1920—   )
is certainly the best.

In his five collections of stories published within an eight-year period—*Dark
Carnival* (1947), *The Martian Chronicles* (1950), *The Illustrated Man* (1951), *The Golden
Apples of the Sun* (1953), *The October Country* (1955)—Bradbury treats the
achievements of science as fable, prophecy, and nightmare. In his satiric
delineation of American society, he sees the dangers emerging from its depen-
dence on machines. His stories satirize those who are ecologically irresponsible,
smug, and materialistic, and he projects the alienation and loneliness he fears
will be a result of these attitudes. Bradbury's fictional realm is one in which
doubt and fear of death produce irrational behavior.

In the opening of *The October Country,* he describes what becomes for him an
eerie world, a country "composed in the main of cellars, sub-cellars, coalbins,
closets, attics, and pantries faced away from the sun . . . whose people passing at
night in the empty walks sound like rain . . ." It is apparent in the tattoos of the
Illustrated Man that this country is the product of our unmasked fears. In this
collection of stories, probably Bradbury's best, the narrator meets a man whose
tattoos are illustrations that "predict the future." As the narrator gazes at the
illustrations, eighteen of them take on life of their own, and from them stories
emerge, each one revealing glimpses of the future. In the epilogue, when the
tales are complete, the narrator sees on the man's back a final scene: "I saw only
enough of the Illustration to make me leap up. . . . The picture on his back
showed the Illustrated Man himself, with his fingers around my neck, choking
me to death." The collection ends with the narrator running toward town,
never looking back.

The rise of science fiction in this period is important in helping shape the
short story of the 1960s and 1970s. Because it created new myths of America,
and because it relied on satire as its chief mode, later writers used many of its
techniques in their innovative fiction.

• • •

Besides science fiction, literature written by blacks was to have a profound
impact on the stories of later decades. One of the most promising black writers
was Langston Hughes (1902—1967). His collection, *Laughing to Keep from Crying*
(1952), is a series of sketches portraying the black experience in America.
Hughes's tales are short and autobiographical, and they reveal a sensitivity to
issues that were beginning to take hold of the national conscience in the 1950s.

In "Who's Passing for Who," the first of the twenty-four sketches, Hughes
begins by writing, "One of the great difficulties about being a member of a

minority race is that so many kindhearted, well-meaning bores gather round to help." This opening is symptomatic of the misunderstanding and tensions Hughes portrays as blacks began their quest for equality. Throughout the collection, "well-meaning bores" are contrasted with intolerant and activist whites and blacks. In "African Morning," Maurai, a mulatto boy, realizes that "nobody wanted him" because he is neither white nor black; in "Something in Common," a black and a white soldier join ranks to fight against their common enemy, prejudice; in "Who's Passing for Who," a man and wife pose as whites, then blacks, then whites again in a comedy of errors. All the stories reveal Hughes's satiric attempts to reconcile the differences between the races. His portraits mark him as one of the important writers of the postwar ear.

• • •

For writers such as Langston Hughes and others who had their start in the decade following the war, the critical reception today is mixed. In part, it is because some of them are seen as imitators of the short story tradition of the first half century or as unsuccessful innovators who were perhaps ahead of their time. Yet the very best of them were and are models of the technical and stylistic virtuosity that mark the development of the twentieth-century short story as a distinctive American achievement. Whether these postwar storytellers used the city or the country as their milieu, the urbane witticisms of New Yorkers or the colloquialisms of Southerners to delineate character, or simply the diversity of American regionalisms and rituals to create their own fictional settings in or out of this world, no simple classifications or generalizations can be applied to any of these major contemporary writers. The individuality of their styles and approaches makes each a special problem in analysis and appreciation.

Yet each of these writers has one thing in common. Each wrote fiction to seek positive values to take the place of those lost in the chaos of the Depression and the Second World War. They recognized that the individual, confronted by the myriad changes that were taking place, was losing his identity and his importance as a person. This search certainly contributed to the starkness and reality of their short stories. For some, this meant writing fiction without departing from the traditional plot framework and creating interest through the interaction of character and incident. For the majority of others, however, the challenge of presenting a portrait of the human scene with sharpened insight and with individually developed styles of their own enabled them to produce stories ranging in mode from the realistic to the allegorical and grotesque. In breaking new ground, these postwar writers worked in the

characteristic American vein, which has always been innovative and explor-
atory, in their attempt to portray the manners of a changing American society.

Jeffrey Walker

Oklahoma State University

1957—1968:
TOWARD DIVERSITY
OF FORM

The period from 1957 to 1968 was an extremely significant and productive one for American practitioners of the art of short fiction. It saw the literary maturation of such major figures as John Cheever, Flannery O'Connor, Isaac Bashevis Singer, and Peter Taylor. It witnessed the emergence of the new and important voices of John Updike, Bernard Malamud, and John Barth.

In the tradition of Hawthorne, James, and Twain, American short-story writers continued to evoke a sense of place in their fiction. Authors such as Cheever, Updike, and Hortense Calisher began to explore what was rapidly becoming a Northeastern megalopolis. The Southern renaissance was in full swing. Other writers in the Midwest and Southwest drew heavily on the cultural background of their regions.

Ethnic heritage was also becoming a very important element in the creative process. In the late 1960s, a number of young writers initiated a black literary renaissance, reconciling their particular concerns with the demands of their craft. It was a synthesis that had already been achieved by Jewish-Americans such as Singer, Malamud, and Saul Bellow who, from the 1950s on, became not only the voices of their own ethnic ties but also ethical spokesmen for American society as a whole.

While it drew on such a variety of backgrounds, the American short story remained, for the most part, a vehicle for the exploration of contemporary society. Indeed, in the 1950s and early 1960s it became apparent that the main purpose of the genre was to create a fiction of manners. This was emphasized by the continued preeminence of periodicals such as *The New Yorker* and the popularity of authors such as Cheever and Updike. Whether they were Easterners or Southerners, Jewish or black Americans, writers in the period contributed to the Jamesian goal of rendering even the "simplest surface" in order "to guess the unseen from the seen, to trace the implication of things, to judge the whole piece by the pattern" (Henry James, "The Art of Fiction").

This is not to suggest that they chose to express contemporary conditions and mores in ways that were completely or even primarily realistic. For, as Richard Chase has suggested in *The American Novel and Its Tradition,* the American imagination "seems less interested in redemption than in the melodrama of the eternal struggle of good and evil, less interested in incarnation and reconcilia- tion" than in "the aesthetic possibilities of radical forms of alienation, con- tradiction and disorder." Embodying these tendencies, the American short story, like the American novel, has often fused realism and romance, something that is particularly evident in the period we are considering.

Faced with the radical changes of the previous few decades, with the growing complexity of contemporary life, the increasingly perplexing relation- ships between the individual and society, short-story writers in the late 1950s and the 1960s began more and more to discover the limitations of realistic or naturalistic fiction. Thus while some continued to focus on the everyday and the usual, others came more and more to explore the grotesque, the fantastic, and the supernatural. While some continued to employ traditional narrative forms, others began not only to reject conventional realistic narrative but also to expose and question the conventions of fiction in general. This blend of realism and romance, of traditional and innovative, characteristic of the fiction of the period as a whole, is manifested even in the work of artists, such as John Cheever, who have somewhat fallaciously been labeled as celebrators and historians of the usual.

• • •

John Cheever (1912—1982) has long been regarded as one of the most astute observers and recorders of contemporary American society. With the publica- tion of *The Stories of John Cheever* (1978) his short fiction won even wider consideration. So polished is his prose for the most part, that it is easy to miss his experimentation with narrative technique and to conclude that he is a mere chronicler of everyday events. So felicitously does he capture the seriocomic essence of metropolitan and suburban angst that one may fail to notice the mythic and fantastic elements interwoven with his observations on contempo- rary mores.

Raised in Quincy, Massachusetts, and having resided in New York and New England, Cheever has much in common with those other products and portrayers of Northeastern culture, Henry James and Nathaniel Hawthorne. Like James he is interested in capturing the intricate vagaries of interpersonal relationships and in exploring the possibilities of fictional narration. While he is not above celebrating the simple joys of life, Cheever, like both these predecessors, is also concerned with that deeper, darker, Puritan aspect of the American psyche, the realm of the moral, mythical, and supernatural. As he himself put it in the Preface to his collected stories: "The constants that I look for in this sometimes dated paraphernalia are a love of light and a determination to trace some moral chain of being. Calvin played no part at all in my religious education, but his presence seemed to abide in the barns of my childhood and to have left me with some undue bitterness." Although Cheever may thus be seen as working within a tradition, both the method and milieu of his short stories are unique and modern, something readily discernible in his first major collection, *The Enormous Radio and Other Stories* (1953).

The differences between the stories in *The Enormous Radio* and his first volume, *The Way Some People Live* (1943), are significant. Impressive as first efforts, the earlier pieces are nonetheless sketchy and sometimes banally realistic (Cheever has called them "embarrassingly immature"). By contrast, the works in his second collection are in every sense more complete and distinctive. Cheever's perennial topics—loneliness, the vanity of human wishes, the evil that conceals itself behind a commonplace facade—are given fuller and more complex treatment. Cheever's mature method, his subtle obfuscation of the realistic and the romantic, is here evident for the first time. Because he has narrowed his geographic compass to New York and its environs, he develops that rich sense of place so crucial to his purpose.

The title story is in many ways illustrative of the book as a whole. Like Paul Hollis of "The Summer Farmer" and the narrator of "The Season of Divorce," Jim and Irene Westcott, the apartment-dwellers in "The Enormous Radio," have purchased happiness with ignorance and self-deception. "The kind of people who seem to strike that satisfactory average of income, endeavor, and respectability that is reached by the statistical reports in college alumni bulletins," the Westcotts become characters in a modern gothic tale, their shallow complacency annihilated by the acquisition of a minor technological marvel. Whether it is a supernatural agent or an objective correlative for the evil and meanness lurking behind the metropolitan mask, their malevolently glowing radio plays out the cruel and shabby dramas that actually are being enacted in the apartments about them. Although they have the radio repaired, they themselves remain permanently attuned to what is "horrible," "dreadful," and "depressing" in their neighbors' lives, aware now that their own life is no different.

Most of the pieces in the collection follow this pattern, the gradual stripping away of illusion, innocence, and ignorance. For many of Cheever's characters, greater awareness brings pain, or even horror, and a heightened sense of futility. In "Torch Song," Jack Lorey discovers too late that a "handsome," "healthy" girl is in reality an Angel of Death with an uncanny, almost supernatural ability to attach herself to men who, like him, are self-destructive and dying. In one of the alternative endings for "O City of Broken Dreams," the Malloys, having been disillusioned by and made to feel ridiculous in New York, head stolidly for California, where presumably they will be disillusioned and made to feel ridiculous once more.

Knowledge is not always a liability, however, and there are moments of light here as well. In "The Pot of Gold," Ralph Whittemore, thwarted in his attempts to acquire wealth, discovers in his wife the treasure he has been seeking. In one of Cheever's best stories, "Goodbye, My Brother," the narrator, maintaining his sense of life in the face of his brother's dark negativism, speaks to us directly and calls our attention to the "surface beauty of life" manifested in a single instant of brightness and perfection.

Cheever's third volume of stories, *The Housebreaker of Shady Hill* (1958), is marked by even greater geographic focus and thematic unity. All of the major characters are residents of the banlieue of Shady Hill, rich or apparently rich suburbanites who "travel around the world, listen to good music, and given a choice of paper books at an airport, will pick Thucydides, and sometimes Aquinas." Most of their stories are expressions of Cheever's belief that "we are still experimenting. This is a haunted nation. Haunted by a dream of excellence."

In Shady Hill the experiment seems to have gone awry; the dream has taken on the qualities of nightmare. We meet a respectable citizen who pilfers cash from his neighbors' homes to keep up appearances, a former track star compelled to relive "his brillant past" by hurdling living room furniture, a "country husband" who discovers Venus in his children's babysitter, and an alcoholic father who cannot understand why his twelve-year-old daughter failed to find "that home sweet home was the best place of all." Excellence has been replaced by status or materialism or security; the power of the dream remains, but Cheever's people seem unable to discover how to embody it.

Cheever's own experimentation, however, is more successful. Many of the stories are characterized by shifts in point of view and by narrative complexity. Reading "The Country Husband" for the first time, for example, we may recognize that something unusual is going on in the first line ("To begin at the beginning . . ."), may even realize that we are to think in terms of oral storytelling. Only when we have read the story through and have experienced Francis Weed's frustration at being unable to recount the crash landing he has survived do we understand that his desire to tell his story in his way has infected the text, making what first appeared as objective narration into something very different.

Whereas Cheever's tapestry of Shady Hill is tightly woven, *Some People, Places, and Things that Will Not Appear in My Next Novel* (1961) is, as the title of one of its pieces suggests, "A Miscellany." Developing a sense of place seems not as important as exploring a variety of reactions to the absurdity and dislocations of contemporary life, and Cheever employs a number of different settings, European as well as American. Most critics citing "A Miscellany of Characters" agree that this is a transitional volume in which Cheever in a sense exorcises unsatisfactory responses to and treatments of the modern condition. Although this may indeed be true, the book as a whole makes clear what will happen in his future work. We find in these pieces a great deal of narrative intrusion and play, a disregard for the restrictions of genre (is "A Miscellany" an essay, a short story, or a blend of both?), and an increasing emphasis on the fantastic and fabulous, all characteristics of the work that follows.

In the closing line of "A Miscellany" Cheever, by implication, makes a commitment "to celebrate a world that lies spread out around us like a bewildering and stupendous dream." In his next book of stories, *The Brigadier and the Golf Widow* (1964), we travel through an America in which the real and the unreal, suburban and dream landscapes, coexist and interpenetrate. In "The Swimmer," for instance, Cheever cleverly confounds internal time, clock time, and mythic time. To Neddy Merrill, his cross-country swim through backyard swimming pools seems to take but an afternoon. There is much textual evidence that suggests, however, that his "heroic journey" begins in midsummer and ends in autumn, and we cannot even be certain whether the seasons through which we move are those of a single year or a lifetime. The reader seeking a rational explanation may find one in the deterioration of Merrill's psychological state, but the mythic structure makes possible another, not necessarily contradictory, reading: Merrill's suburban *nostos* is an ironic odyssey that results in loss of social status and concludes with his return to a locked and deserted home.

Cheever's use of apparently realistic narration to achieve surrealistic effects is also evident in this collection. In two stories, the dream world intrudes in the form of seemingly supernatural agents who offer assistance to his afflicted suburbanites. In "The Angel of the Bridge," a hitchhiking angel intercedes to help the narrator overcome his phobia about bridges, a fear linked to his hatred of modern life. In "The Music Teacher," a modern-day witch provides a harried husband with a musical formula that converts his wife from shrew to slave. In the four sketches that comprise "Metamorphoses," he concocts a playful mixture of fantasy and irony, matter-of-factly describing a series of modern ovidian transformations that comment not only on the diminution of humans but also on the deflation of myth itself.

If *The Brigadier and the Golf Widow* is dominated by one impulse in Cheever's fiction, the reaction to calvinism, the descent into bitterness, then *The World of Apples* (1974) contains some of the clearest expressions of that other, contrary impulse, the celebration of living, the ascent into light. This is not to say that Cheever has put failure, frustration, and loss behind him; they are still inextricably bound up in the contemporary condition. But one may discover in several of these stories a change in tone, an aura of affirmation. Perhaps the best example of this is the well-crafted title story, which recounts the struggle of a poet to overcome the fading of inspiration and the feeling that his work has been unjustly overlooked. Although he succumbs for a time to the downward pull, indulging in suicidal thoughts and scatological verse, he checks his fall, purifies himself through nature and memory, and begins "a long poem on the inalienable dignity of light and air." It is a fitting conclusion to the final story in the final volume that Cheever produced in the period.

•   •   •

Born in Shillington, Pennsylvania, and educated at Harvard, John Updike (1932—   ) is, like Cheever, a Northeasterner whose fiction ostensibly records the everyday lives of ordinary people in small-town, urban, and suburban America. Also like Cheever, Updike is a master craftsman, a novelist as well as a short-story writer, whose short fiction has most often appeared in *The New Yorker.* Whereas Cheever's genii are James and Hawthorne, Updike's genius is clearly James Joyce.

In his childhood reminiscences, "A Dogwood Tree," Updike presents an approach to art which he tells us he has never outgrown:

I reasoned thus: just as the paper is the basis for the marks upon it, might not events be contingent upon a never-expressed (because featureless) ground? Is the true marvel of Sunday skaters the pattern of their pirouettes or the fact that they are silently upheld? Blankness is not emptiness; we may skate upon an intense radiance we do not see because we see nothing else. And in fact there is a color, a quiet but tireless goodness that things at rest, like a brick wall or a small stone, seem to affirm. A wordless reassurance these things are pressing to give. An hallucination? To transcribe middleness with all its grits, bumps, and anonymities, in its fullness of satisfaction and mystery: is it possible or, in view of the suffering that violently colors the periphery and that at all moments threatens to move into the center, worth doing?

It is a statement of purpose that has much in common with the esthetic theory in Joyce's own book of reminiscences, *Stephen Hero.*

Updike's commitment "to transcribe middleness," then, is a commitment to seeing clearly and fully, to capturing all of the complex "pirouettes" of life in order ultimately to apprehend that radiant goodness that brings reassurance. Thus the typical Updike story, like the typical *Dubliners* story, is dependent for its effect not on overt action but on the accumulation of details and perceptions leading to that moment of epiphany when we see beyond the chaotic surface of things. There is, however, a distinctive difference between Joyce's short fiction and Updike's.

In Joyce's dark Dublin, to see clearly is usually to apprehend folly, frustration, or loss, to become aware of the tangled snares woven by self and circumstance. Although this is true of many of Updike's pieces as well, his epiphanies are occasionally more positive. For him, *claritas* sometimes truly is *quidditas,* and the light does shine through.

This careful balancing of the delineation of life's grits and bumps with intuition of its satisfactions and mysteries is found in Updike's first volume of stories, *The Same Door* (1959). In this collection we discover characters who exhibit an entire spectrum of responses to revelation. In "Tomorrow and Tomorrow and So Forth," Mark Prosser makes a conscious effort to disregard his moment of insight, to hold on to the illusion of self-importance rather than admit to himself that he, like his more ordinary colleagues, has been ridiculed by two of his high school students. In another story, "Sunday Teasing," a somewhat similar character does permit himself to see a bit more clearly, allowing one day's events to coalesce into the realization that he doesn't "know anything." Although it is unclear whether or not he will act on the self-knowledge he has gained, move beyond tolerance of his wife's ignorance to an acceptance of her difference, we cannot help but feel that his reaction is in some way more positive than Prosser's.

Finally, in "Dentistry and Doubt," an American cleric visiting England possesses a moment that qualifies as an epiphany in its fullest sense. Sitting in the dentist's chair and feeling disoriented and isolated, Burton is troubled by his own skepticism and by the presence of evil in the world. Overcoming difficulties of communication, however, he reaches out to the dentist and is rewarded, in this most incongruous of settings, with a vision of universal harmony: "Outside the window, the wrens and starlings, mixed indistinguishably, engaged in maneuvers that seemed essentially playful."

Updike's next two volumes of stories, *Pigeon Feathers* (1962) and *Olinger Stories: A Selection* (1964), make clear something that is perhaps not initially apparent in *The Same Door:* for Updike, experience is not only a balance of positive and negative discoveries, but a mixture of "memory and desire." Updike chose as the epigraph for *Pigeon Feathers* a passage from Kafka's "A Report to an Academy," which reads, in part: "In revenge, however, my memory of the past has closed the door against me more and more. I could have returned at first, had human beings allowed it, through an archway as wide as the span of heaven over the earth, but as I spurred myself on in my forced career, the opening narrowed and shrank behind me; I felt more comfortable in the world of men and fitted it better."

Viewed in terms of this epigraph, Updike's early stories fall into two basic categories, those that are products of an attempt to recapture, through memory, the innocent joys and gropings of youth, and those that describe the efforts of older individuals to reach outward into "the world of men" in search of mature joys. A careful reading of *Olinger Stories,* which collects all of the Olinger pieces from the first two volumes (Olinger is Updike's fictional shadow of Shillington, Pennsylvania), reveals an increasing distancing from that childhood world. The epigraph to *Pigeon Feathers* and the Olinger collection both emphasize not only the importance to Updike of recapturing the past, but his growing difficulty in sustaining that nostalgic impulse in the face of more so-called adult concerns.

This becomes especially significant when one realizes that the majority of positive epiphanies in *Pigeon Feathers* take place in the past, a past that is as much recreated through art and conscious effort as it is recollected. The epiphanies recorded in stories such as "A Sense of Shelter" and "Pigeon Feathers" seem more temporary, become moments of insight and satisfaction that mark a journey outward. At the same time, the stories with more contemporary settings ("Walter Briggs," "Dear Alexandros," "The Doctor's Wife") become increasingly marked by a perception of separation and an awareness of the gulfs between past and present, self and others.

"The Persistence of Desire" is in many ways the most characteristic story of this stage in Updike's career. A young man, changed by the world (a magazine article he reads proclaims, "the cells of the human body are replaced in toto every seven years"), returns to Olinger. In an optometrist's office, amid a stopped grandfather clock and "other imitation antiques," he encounters a former sweetheart. He tells her that he is happily married, "but happiness isn't everything," and filled with the memory of past desire, he attempts to arrange an assignation. When he leaves the office, however, he discovers that he cannot read the note she has passed him, for time has dismissed him "into a tainted world where things evaded his focus." His desire remains unfulfilled in the present; only in an imagined past can he find satisfaction and clarity of vision: "The maples, macadam, shadows, houses, cement, were to his violated eyes as brilliant as a scene remembered; he became a child again in this town, where life was a distant adventure, a rumor, an always imminent joy."

The initial piece of *The Music School* (1966), the last Updike volume to appear in the period, contains a farewell to Olinger. The tone of "In Football Season" is consciously nostalgic, and the story concludes with the narrator grudgingly pulling himself forward in time: "Now I peek into windows and open doors and do not find that air of permission. It has fled the world. Girls walk by me carrying invisible bouquets from fields still steeped in grace, and I look up in the manner of one who follows with his eyes the passage of a hearse, and remembers what pierces him." One world has died for him, and he must find what he can in another.

As many of the stories in *The Music School* emphasize, that other world, the adult one of marriage and social interaction, is harder, less tolerant, and marked to a great extent by divorce in all its forms. Updike's contemporary characters sleep in separate beds ("Twin Beds in Rome"), suspect each other of infidelity ("The Rescue"), and purchase what happiness they have with blood ("Giving Blood"). Speaking of his earlier work in the Foreword to *Olinger Stories,* Updike noted that the point of them was that "*We are* rewarded *unexpectedly. The* muddled and inconsequent surface of things now and then parts to yield us a gift." In *The Music School,* there are few such gratuitous gifts; whatever has been gained has usually been paid for.

Updike does not, however, permit suffering permanently to usurp the center. In the title story, for example, we share with Alfred Schweigen an epiphany in some ways fuller and more significant than those that dot the enchanted landscape of memory. Surrounded by indifference and diffidence, Schweigen is a writer who cannot write, adrift in a modern limbo: "We are all pilgrims, faltering toward divorce. Some get no further than mutual confession, which becomes an addiction, and exhausts them. Some move on, into violent quarrels and physical blows; and succumb to sexual excitement. A few make it to the psychiatrists. A very few get as far as the lawyers." Technology, the substitute for religion, provides him with no solution, for it has merely replaced one kind of acolyte with another, the "typical specimen of the new human species that thrives around scientific centers, in an environment of discussion groups, outdoor exercise, and cheerful husbandry."

Yet in spite of all this, Schweigen, with the aid of the synthesizing power of music, experiences a moment of satisfaction through a hard-won acceptance of life as it is: "The world is the host; it must be chewed. I am content here in this school. My daughter emerges from her lesson. Her face is fat and satisfied, refreshed, hopeful; her pleased smile, biting her lower lip, pierces my heart and I die (I think I am dying) at her feet."

The intensity and the holistic quality of Schweigen's experience here illustrate why there is little of the supernatural in Updike's short fiction. For him, the natural and supernatural are not coexistent. The spiritual is bound up with the material; the luminous essence of things shines through them to be perceived in instants of heightened perception. Whether Updike's stories culminate in major epiphanies or conclude with lesser, more equivocal ones, their success or failure depends, therefore, not solely on the development of patterns of images, but on his ability to convey a flash of intuition in a few highly charged words.

This may be one of the things responsible for what some perceive as an unevenness in his work. When we feel that the *mots justes* have evaded him at the crucial point, the story as a whole may strike us as on the one hand artificial or on the other prosaic. When Updike succeeds, however, the effect is as wonderful as any to be found in the genre.

• • •

The two collections published by Peter Taylor (1917—   ) in the late 1950s and early 1960s attest to his continued mastery of the form. The sense of place remains strong in these stories, most of which are set in the country towns and cities of contemporary Tennessee. Taylor is certainly more than a regional writer, however. Less of an experimentalist than Cheever, less a modernist than Updike, he is nonetheless their equal in technical artistry, and he shares with them some basic concerns: the subtleties of interpersonal relationships, the difficulty of communication, and the effects of urbanization on individuals and their culture.

The title of Taylor's third volume, *Happy Families Are all Alike* (1959), taken from *Anna Karenina* ("Happy families are all alike; every unhappy family is unhappy in its own way"), emphasizes once more his preoccupation with home life as mirror of the contemporary condition.

In "Heads of Houses," he adroitly manipulates point of view to delineate the intricacies of familial stratagems and alliances. Although Taylor's technique here is certainly not innovative, the story is a tour de force, a smooth and masterful evocation of the manner in which preconceptions and failed communication may negate good intentions and blind a household to its potential sources of strength and harmony. Whereas here the combatants are male heads of houses, in "Guests" it is the women, Henrietta and her country cousin, Annie, who engage in warfare with social convention for weapons, making it impossible for the men to reach out to one another in hope of discovering "what it is people keep alive for."

Taylor's characters may be ordinary people and the world they inhabit the everyday world, but there is an undercurrent of evil and a trace of the supernatural in many of his stories that place them in the tradition of Southern gothic. "A Walled Garden," for example, is a cameo of evil incarnate, reminiscent in setting of Hawthorne's "Rappaccini's Daughter" and in technique of

Browning's "My Last Duchess." Through dramatic monologue, Mrs. Harris reveals to us how her insane desire for control and order led her cruelly and unfeelingly to prune her daughter's spirit and individuality so that she, too, might fit into the scheme of her mother's walled garden. In Taylor's 1959 O. Henry Award winner, "Venus, Cupid, Folly, and Time," narrative complexity, intimations of incest, and careful development of atmosphere contribute to an eerie yet poignant portrayal of decay.

Taylor's fondness for the supernatural, the slightly surreal, and the grotesque is further evident in three of the previously uncollected pieces that appear in *Miss Leonora when Last Seen* (1963), a volume of sixteen stories, ten of which appeared in *The Widows of Thornton* and *A Long Fourth*. One of these stories, entitled, appropriately enough, "A Strange Story," deals overtly with the apparently supernatural, with the narrator's recollections of a period in his childhood when the world was a magical place in which mysterious, quixotic, and sometimes prophetic voices spoke to him. In another, "At the Drugstore," Matt Donelson, "back home on a visit," wakes up one morning and walks, apparently unconsciously, to a neighborhood drugstore where he seems to step back in time: "It was as if this very morning he had run all the way from home with his school books under one arm and his yellow slicker under the other and was now afraid that the streetcar—the good old Country Day Special—would pass before he could get waited on." The face behind the drugstore counter is "indisputably the face of old Mr. Conway as it had been forty years ago," the now modern drugstore threatens "to turn back into the place it had been once," and Matt feels trapped "in a dream from which he could not wake himself."

There are, of course, psychological explanations for the occurrences in both these stories. The narrator of "A Strange Story" merely thinks he heard voices, something not uncharacteristic of certain children at a certain stage of development. Matt sees what he wants to see in the drugstore so that he can fulfill a subconscious need to clarify his roles as son and father. Taylor's skillful use of point of view, however, makes it difficult for us to be satisfied with such analysis. So clever is he at making us imagine that we hear what a character hears or see what he sees, that even after the fact, when the common-sense alternatives become apparent (the figure behind the counter is Conway's son), we are still left with the feeling that we have experienced something unusual. Like Cheever in "The Swimmer" or James in "The Turn of the Screw," Taylor leaves us suspended somewhere between the rational and the supernatural.

In the title story Taylor plays on our conceptions of what is realistic or normal in a slightly different manner. Miss Leonora Logan appears at first to be a type—the small-town eccentric, regarded by other townspeople as slightly peculiar in behavior and dress. The last surviving member of "a family that for a hundred years did all it could to impede the growth and progress" of her town, she is a living anachronism, the final existing specimen of an outmoded way of life.

Again, Taylor makes us uneasy in our attempts to categorize and define. Miss Leonora is a grotesque only in the eyes of those around her, among whom we cannot count the narrator. His ambivalence toward her, in fact, leads us to consider the inherent relativism of concepts such as conformity and sanity. Even more than that, his inability or unwillingness to tell us her whereabouts calls into question our very notions of reality itself. All we have are a few tantalizing documents, a half-dozen postcards, to trace her existence in space and time, and the narrator's belief, perhaps the product of his need to believe, that she is still alive behind the wheel of her 1942 Dodge convertible, "orbiting her native state." She remains, finally, an intuited but unseen presence some-where "out there," and readers may consider, if just for a moment, to what extent their own sense of people and things is based on similarly dubious bits of evidence.

If we are even slightly unsure about something that fundamental, can we wholeheartedly agree with the narrator that "times do change, and the interests of one individual cannot be allowed to hinder the progress of a whole community"? Can we be certain that Miss Leonora's opposition to the con-demnation of Logana and the community's plans for "a new consolidated high school" is the product of individual interests alone? We most likely cannot, and Taylor here, as elsewhere, is asking us to consider the nature of change, the relationship of the past to the present. These are complex matters, and his awareness of relativism prevents Taylor from presenting us with facile formula-tions. As a native of a state that is neither Southern nor Midwestern, a member of a society that is a mixture of the old elegance and the new commercialism, he can do no more or less than convey to us what it means to be, like Miss Leonora and Thomasville itself, suspended between.

• • •

Although Tillie Olsen (1913—   ) shares with Taylor a profound interest in the complexities of familial relationships, her approach is significantly different. Taylor is extremely adept at using the conventional tools of third-person narrative and dialogue to create the illusion of intimacy with his characters, but something is always withheld from us. Even when he occasionally employs first-person narrative, we are still being "told" a story, and we are never actually privy to his characters' innermost thoughts and impressions. In con-trast, Olsen's technique is an innovative combination of third-person narrative, dialogue, and interior monologue that reveals her characters' thoughts, memories, and perceptions. Many of Taylor's stories expand outward from dialogue to atmosphere; all of Olsen's move from dialogue inward, focusing on individual instants of experience.

The extreme care with which Olsen practices her art is attested to by the fact that her complete fictional oeuvre consists of four short stories and one short novel. Although this might lead one to assume that she is a limited writer, nothing could be farther from the truth. Each of the stories in *Tell Me a Riddle* (1961) is a minor masterpiece, and the characters whose inner lives are explored are vastly different individuals, similar only in their preoccupation with isolation and regret. Whether depicting a mother's attempts to rationalize her neglect of her daughter ("I Stand here Ironing"), a merchant seaman's self-destructive ambivalence toward family and security ("Hey Sailor, What Ship?"), or a young girl's initiation into the cold truths of social reality ("O Yes"), Olsen time and again discovers the universal in the particular.

The method of the title story is typical. Dying of cancer, an old woman stubbornly resists the half-selfish efforts of her family to convince her to go quietly and peacefully. Refusing to play the role of transmitter of tradition, she recoils, folds in on herself:

Blows, screams, a call: "Grandma!" For her? Oh please not for her. Hide, hunch behind the dresses deeper. But a trembling little body hurls itself beside her—surprised, smothered laughter, arms surround her neck, tears rub dry on her cheeks, and words too soft to understand whisper into her ear (Is this where you hide too, Grammy? It's my secret place, we have a secret now).
And the sweat beads, and the long shudder seizes.

When she does begin to speak, it is to spew out a torrent of "stained words" that "betray" her "youth of belief" and indict the times in which she has lived. Although her husband tries not to listen to her, he is forced into an awareness of her suffering and his own:

The cards fell from his fingers. Without warning, the bereavement and betrayal he had sheltered—compounded through the years—hidden even from himself—revealed itself,
uncoiled,
released,
sprung

and with it the monstrous shapes of what had actually happened in the century.

For Olsen, to be conscious is to live with pain; she captures one individual's private agony, and through it portrays the torment of a generation.

• • •

Like Olsen, John Knowles (1926—   ) published only one collection in the period, but the six stories in *Phineas* (1968) are also worthy of note, and he manifests a good deal of variety in his treatments of contemporary individuals and society. Two of the stories take place at Devon School, the setting of his popular novel, *A Separate Peace*. (Indeed, "Phineas" is a different version of the central incident in that novel.) The others are set in such widely divergent places as West Virginia; Wetherford, Connecticut; Cairo; and St. Jean de Luz, France. Through their day-to-day interactions, Knowles's characters reveal their self-centeredness, jealousy, and potential for evil.

Knowles is at his best when he injects an almost vicious irony into his character sketches, and plays on the reader's expectations. In "The Peeping Tom," for example, Paul Marowski's antisocial behavior is motivated by his inability to replace his father and fit into the female-dominated universe of his own home. Brought to trial, he views his public humiliation as a form of salvation, a means of "getting out" of "the trap" his life has become. "A Turn with the Sun," perhaps the best piece in the volume, hinges on a stunning reversal. Wanting desperately to fit into the society of Devon School, Lawrence Stuart first attempts to win the respect of the school's elite. Failing miserably, he tries to satisfy his egotism by excelling in his studies and playing the contemptuous loner to become "the greatest, and the most inaccessible." Gradually, he begins to realize his folly, to discover the finitude of life, the transience of fame. The universe remains as indifferent to him as it ever was. In the fullness of his new-found self-knowledge he drowns, while the seasons move on, and "the earth, turned full toward the sun," brings "forth its annual harvest."

•   •   •

Whereas Olsen and Knowles are examples of the writer who can exhibit a good deal of versatility in a few short pieces, John O'Hara (1905—1970) is a prime example of the veteran writer who, settling into a style, can play a seemingly infinite number of variations on a limited number of themes and character types. Following a fourteen-year hiatus, during which time he wrote novels, plays, and essays, but no short stories, O'Hara rediscovered the genre, producing a body of work that attests to his incredible prolificacy. Between 1960 and his death in 1970, he published six large volumes of stories: *Assembly* (1960), *The Cape Cod Lighter* (1962), *The Hat on the Bed* (1963), *The Horse Knows the Way* (1964), *Waiting for Winter* (1966), and *And Other Stories* (1969). Two other volumes, *The Time Element* (1972) and *The O'Hara Generation* (1972), a retrospective, were published posthumously.

Turning his reporter's eye on the society of the 1960s, O'Hara updates the chronicle of American life begun in his short fiction of the 1930s and 1940s. His themes are the perennial ones of loneliness, the war between the sexes, difficulties of aging, and the ephemerality of success. His characters usually survive as best they can, considering their diminished potential, in a society that is indifferent to individual wants and intolerant of individual differences.

O'Hara has often been criticized as being a formula writer, a popular author whose work is essentially nonliterary. It may be partially true, as Albert Erskine suggests in the Introduction to *The O'Hara Generation,* that this evaluation is a fiction concocted by reviewers and members of the academic community who are unable to recognize excellence in any popular writer. There is no denying that what O'Hara does, he does well. Nonetheless, anyone who reads a significant number of his stories cannot help but begin to notice a remarkable sameness to them. Coming to know O'Hara is coming to know what to expect.

· · ·

Irwin Shaw (1913—   ) is another popular writer who was quite productive in the period, publishing three collections: *Tip on a Dead Jockey and Other Stories* (1957), *Love on a Dark Street and Other Stories* (1965), and *Short Stories* (1966). At his worst, Shaw vacillates between the banal and the sensational, and the strings he pulls are often too obvious. At his best, in stories such as "Love on a Dark Street" and "Circle of Light," he effectively evokes the anomic nature of contemporary life in the big cities and affluent suburbs of Europe and America.

· · ·

The characters we encounter in Gilbert Rogin's *The Fencing Master* (1965) are, like many of O'Hara's and Shaw's anti-heroes, unexceptional men who feel put upon by existence itself, and are unable or just barely able to cope with the daily pressures of making a living and maintaining social relationships. Whether the setting is New York, Miami, Las Vegas, Los Angeles, or even the South Pacific, when we read one of Rogin's stories we are thrust into a neurotic universe in which even dreams are indictments. Constantly psychoanalyzing himself and evaluating his own motives and deeds, the typical Rogin protagonist is incapable of acting. Many of the most important literary works of the century have dealt with this aspect of the modern condition.

For Shaw and Rogin, the significant elements of urban existence are the same everywhere. Their characters move through a paradigmatic metropolis that bears many names. In the works of Richard Yates, Louis Auchincloss, and Hortense Calisher, the city is more specifically New York.

· · ·

The New Yorkers to whom Richard Yates (1926—   ) introduces us in *Eleven Kinds of Loneliness* (1962) are members of the middle and lower middle class—cab drivers, newspapermen, school teachers, young couples starting out in life. All experience some kind of loneliness; some attempt to find self-definition and overcome their isolation by reaching out to others, acquiring possessions, or pursuing what they think of as success. In one story, "The B.A.R. Man," the search for self-esteem, following a pattern that has become increasingly common, leads to an act of irrational violence. John Fallon, a clerk for an insurance company, is a man "nobody had even thought much about" until "he got his name on the police blotter, and in the papers." Aging, his job and home life dull routines, Fallon still wears his "serviceman's identification bracelet, the relic of a braver and more careless time," and his only source of pride is the memory that he had been pronounced "a damn good B.A.R. man" during the war. Thwarted and mocked in the present, he strikes out at a political figure who becomes, purely by accident, the focus for his rage and frustration.

• • •

In *Powers of Attorney* (1963) and *Tales of Manhattan* (1967), Louis Auchincloss (1917—   ) introduces us to a different class of people—the patrons of "the ancient auction gallery of Philip Hone & Sons," members of the respected law firm of Arnold & Degener, society matrons who hold court in Manhattan and Oyster Bay. Auchincloss's work is perhaps the clearest example of the short fiction of manners to be produced in the period. Although he has been taken to task for the uniformity of his approach and the triviality of his subject matter, *Tales of Manhattan* demonstrates his ability to manipulate point of view and his willingness to inject a touch of the bizarre or supernatural into his urbane universe. Exhibiting his characteristic wit and sophistication, both these collections contribute significantly to Auchincloss's objective of fully dissecting a particular stratum of society in the manner of an American Trollope or Galsworthy.

• • •

In some ways, the stories of Hortense Calisher (1911—   ) present a more complete portrait of New York and its inhabitants than we find in the work of either Yates or Auchincloss. In *Tale for the Mirror* (1962) and *Extreme Magic* (1963), her second and third collections, we encounter the surviving members of a genteel society that has become anomalous and anachronistic, and the representatives of a younger, urban middle class who discover success, values, and even human relationships to be ephemeral and contingent. Moreover, the city we visit is not only the impersonal contemporary metropolis of the 1960s but the more human and comfortable New York of the 1910s and 1920s.

Through the accumulation of details and the description of objects, places, and everyday rituals, Calisher develops a full and rich sense of place in her fiction. This is particularly true of the Hester-Kinny Elkin stories, which appear in all of her collections and which are based in part on memories of her childhood. Calisher, however, aspires to a good deal more than careful observation of external detail. As she herself notes in the preface to *The Collected Stories of Hortense Calisher* (1975), the "very duration" of the short story, "too brief to make a new mode in, verges it always toward that classical corner where sits the human figure. And perhaps the genre flourishes best during those periods of life—both for authors and eras—when the human drama is easier accepted as the main one going. . . . A story may float like an orb, spread like a fan or strike its parallels ceaselessly on the page—as long as its clues cohere. Language itself may *be* the idea."

Some readers may feel that at times Calisher focuses on scenes of human drama that are too minor to warrant serious consideration. In other stories, her love and mastery of language cause her to approach a kind of verbal preciosity, and the medium of telling threatens to overwhelm the tale. In her most successful pieces, however, she presents full and human characters in fitting and elegant language, elevating the apparently trivial and local to the significant and universal.

· · ·

The development of a sense of place is also an important element in the short fiction of a number of other writers active in the period. This is not to suggest that these authors should be viewed as local colorists, a term that has been applied in the past to such major figures as Hawthorne, Twain, and Faulkner. The evocation of locale should be considered in its relationships to other aspects of their work. Indeed, as we shall see, many of the Midwesterners, Southwesterners, and Southerners contributing to the genre in the years 1957—1968 share the major concerns of those Northeastern regionalists, Cheever and Updike.

The blankness, provinciality, and hermetic family structure of the Midwest figure prominently in the stories of R. V. Cassill (1913—   ), Calvin Kentfield (1925—   ), Evan S. Connell, Jr. (1924—   ), and William H. Gass (1924—   ). The strongest stories in Cassill's *The Father* (1965) and *The Happy Marriage* (1965) are set in Iowa or other parts of the region. "Larchmoor is Not the World," for example, traces with gentle irony the seduction of an English professor by a literary type. Deluding himself, Dr. Cameron ventures out of the safe physical and emotional retreat he has created on a small Midwest campus, enticed by a vision of "the gold-embroidered princess, the beautiful lady without mercy and hope." Drawn out of his "warmer corner," he concludes that he will "die in the real cold," defending himself "against self-ridicule, self-obloquy." In "The Father," a story that is vastly different in both tone and impact, Cassill plays on our superficial conceptions of Midwestern farm life, creating a powerful drama of guilt and obsession that truly qualifies as American gothic.

Kentfield's *The Angel and the Sailor* (1957) and *The Great Wondering Goony Bird* (1963) illustrate both the variety of ways in which a writer can make use of regional heritage and the inadequacy of regionalism as a critical concept. In "The Rose of Sharon" and the stories that highlight the Garrett family ("Chip Canary," "River Stay 'way from My Door") the accurate depiction of small-town life is crucial to Kentfield's exploration of the trials of youth and adolescence. In his fine ghost story, "The Angel and the Sailor," on the other hand, we are made to distrust our sense of place as much as our sense of reality. Merging the real and the supernatural, Kentfield turns a Midwestern farm into a backdrop against which the Strap family plays out its fears and anxieties, wrestling unsuccessfully with mysteries of heredity, until the Iowa landscape and some past ocean appear to coexist in a kind of non-time. Finally, in Kentfield's sea stories, place becomes indistinguishable from character. There is a good deal of Kansas in Davy Humble, the naive merchant seaman who appears in many of these tales, and in "Windmills," another character, drawing on the Midwest that lives in his memory, transforms a waterspout into a tornado and Palermo into the expanses of his boyhood.

Several of the stories in Connell's *The Anatomy Lesson* (1957) satirize Midwestern sterility and provinciality. The title story, for instance, presents the painful and apparently futile attempts of an art professor to awaken his dull, practical students to the sweetness and bitterness of life, while "The Beau Monde of Mrs. Bridge" effectively, if a bit archly, dissects a Kansas City matron who in her innocence, hypocrisy, and pretension has much in common with E. E. Cummings's "Cambridge Ladies." Other pieces in *The Anatomy Lesson* and in Connell's later collection, *At the Crossroads* (1965), however, take place in New York, Rome, Paris, a Nevada desert that could be the set for a Beckett play, and a universe that to all intents and purposes exists only in dialogue.

Although it may seem now to be a bit dated, in retrospect a bit too much a product of the 1960s, W. H. Gass's *In the Heart of the Heart of the Country* (1968) had a significant impact when it was first published and probably influenced a number of young writers. The title story is an excellent example of how far one can progress from the simplistic approach of the nineteenth century local color tale without abandoning, as other contemporary writers have, the sense of a specific place. Using a style that is more lyrical than narrative, and employing the modernist techniques of fragmentation and repetition, Gass obliterates the distinction between inner and outer landscapes. The wintry emotional and mental state of Gass's love-sick narrator is projected onto the environment:

"For we're always out of luck here. That's just how it is—for instance in winter. The sides of the buildings, the roofs, the limbs of the trees are gray. Streets, sidewalks, faces, feelings, they are gray. Speech is gray, and the grass where it shows." At the same time, the weather has its effect on the inner climate: "In the Midwest, around the lower lakes, the sky in the winter is heavy and close, and it is a rare day, a day to remark on, when the sky lifts and allows the heart up." Exploring the possible relationships between the observer and the observed, Gass raises a number of ontological questions while still managing to capture what he considers to be the sterile, mechanical aspects of Midwestern society. Although one may question whether the form he has chosen is adequate for its philosophical content, one must admire the effort.

• • •

In new collections published in the 1960s, William Humphrey (1925—   ) and William Goyen (1915—   ) manifest different approaches to their Southwestern legacies. The title of Humphrey's second collection, *A Time and a Place: Stories of the Red River Country* (1965), reemphasizes the importance of temporal and geographic location in his fiction. All of the stories take place in the Red River Country, the border between Oklahoma and Texas, in the 1930s, the period which marks the death of frontier existence and the birth of the new Southwest. Humphrey focuses on individuals who are affected by the changes in their environment: farmers driven insane with greed by the discovery of oil or native Americans faced with cultural extinction. While some of Humphrey's plots and his use of biblical tone and diction are at times obvious, his work is redeemed by his ability to maintain contact with the "red Oklahoma Earth."

Goyen's *The Faces of Blood Kindred* (1960) is, like his earlier work, characterized by the exploration of different kinds of frontiers—the blurred borders between narrative and lyrical, realistic and mythic or fantastic, material and spiritual. As he points out in the Introduction to the *Selected Writings of William Goyen* (1974), the world of Trinity, Texas, "its countryside, its folk, its speech and superstitions and fable, was stamped into" his senses during his first seven years of life. Although he has lived outside of the region for most of his adult life, his "writing life" has focused upon ways of "giving shape to what happened, of searching for meanings, clarification, Entirety."

Less overtly fantastic than those in *Ghost and Flesh* (1952), the stories in Goyen's second volume examine the claims of the dead on the living, past on the present. Employing a style that melds objective description, lyricism, and personal symbolism, Goyen traces the physical and spiritual ties that bind the individual to something greater than himself. It is a process that does indeed lead to meaning and a sense of "Entirety," for as one of his characters notes, it is "the effect of what was" that "is the long-lastingness in us. . . . The same patterns do exist all over the world. . . . And a sudden sight of this human pattern in one place restores a lost recognition of it in another, far away, through an eternal image of a simple flower, in the hands and care of both . . . "

• • •

While such writers were discovering the fictional possibilities in their Mid-western or Southwestern heritage, others were contributing in remarkably varied ways to the development of what has been called a Southern literary renaissance. John Bell Clayton's *The Strangers Were There* (1957) was published posthumously in the period, as was Flannery O'Connor's *Everything that Rises must Converge* (1965). The year 1963 saw the publication of works as different as *Old Red and Other Stories,* a volume of earlier pieces by Caroline Gordon (1895—1981), and *The Names and Faces of Heroes* by the North Carolinian Reynolds Price (1933—   ). Tennessee Williams's third book of stories, *The Knightly Quest,* appeared in 1967.

• • •

The significance of his Southernness for Florida's George Garrett (1929—   ) is emphasized by the passage from *Jeremiah* 12:8 that serves as the epigraph for one of his pieces: "Mine heritage is unto me as a lion in the forest; it crieth out against me; therefore have I hated it." Many of the stories in *King of the Mountain* (1957), *In the Briar Patch* (1961), and *Cold Ground Was My Bed Last Night* (1964), probe this heritage in its multiple forms: the knowledge and memories a son inherits from his father ("The Test," "The King of the Mountain"), the gentleman's code of behavior that forbids masculine sensitivity ("In the Briar Patch"), and the Southern legacy of violence ("The Last of the Spanish Blood," "Comic Strip"). Although Garrett's heritage may at times cause him anguish, his response never takes the form of lament. His characters, like Professor B. of "Comic Strip," may discover in history a sense of shame, guilt, disgust, and confinement, but Garrett is protected from self-hatred by language and humor.

• • •

Like Garrett, Doris Betts (1932—   ) is very skillful at demonstrating the influence of her cultural milieu on the psychology of ordinary Southerners. Many of the characters in *The Astronomer and Other Stories* (1965) are unremarka-ble people who, confined by their small-town or rural environments and by their own ordinariness, make pathetic, ludicrous, and futile attempts to escape what and where they are. A bored housewife fantasizes about a road crew; a small-town lawyer tries to "make the most of what he has" by orchestrating an

"Egg Day" celebration; a retired mill worker becomes a self-proclaimed astronomer. Through precise prose and careful selection of tone, Betts manages to expose the sexual energy, violence, and despair underlying the surfaces of their lives, while avoiding the cliched sensationalism of the genre to which one of her characters is addicted—those books "about plantations, lusty octoroons, and dueling pistols fired through curtains of Spanish moss."

• • •

The short stories of two other writers, Jesse Stuart (1907—   ) and Donald Windham (1920—   ), once again call into question the concept of regionalism, for they not only exhibit widely different approaches to place, but they also depict two different Souths. An incredibly prolific Kentuckian, Stuart published four collections of stories in the period: *Plowshare in Heaven* (1958), *Save Every Lamb* (1964), *A Jesse Stuart Harvest* (1965), *My Land Has a Voice* (1966). Telling simple tales simply, he has confined himself to the task of celebrating all aspects of his own particular section of rural America. Whereas Stuart writes of the relatively unchanging world of the Kentucky hills in a style that exhibits some of the qualities of oral folklore, Windham writes of the modern urban South in a manner that is a good deal more literary. His Atlanta, recreated in *The Warm Country* (1962) and *Emblems of Conduct* (1963), a book of reminiscences, is probably the farthest thing possible from Stuart's nurturing, responsive land. It is a place that leaves people "deserted, stranded, spent" ("The Warm Country"), and where honor, beauty, and love are elusive ("The Seventh Day"). Failed communication is a major theme in Windham's work, and his characters have difficulty contacting their environment as well as each other. When they do, it is often to read in the landscape a reflection of their own internal condition, as in "Life of Georgia," in which the city sends (in the form of an insurance company sign) a message that seems to mock a young woman's empty, stagnant life.

• • •

Ernest Gaines's South is yet a different place. Although Gaines (1933—   ) has until now produced only a single volume of stories, he has made a significant contribution to the genre. Focusing on the black experience in rural Louisiana, his work is more than history, sociology, or psychology.

Bloodline (1968) is an extremely varied and consistently excellent collection in which Gaines draws on elements of his ethnic and regional heritage and uses a number of different narrative techniques to develop universal themes. In "A Long Day in November," for example, his mastery of first-person narrative (we view things through the eyes of a young boy) and his fine ear for dialogue and dialect combine to produce a strong, unnerving, yet sensitive portrayal of family relationships. In another piece, "Just Like a Tree," he employs multiple points of view, turning the depiction of a single, apparently simple episode into a commentary on the tensions and differences between young and old, past and present, whites and blacks, city-dwellers and country-dwellers.

Gaines's treatment of racial matters is always subtle and complex. "Three Men" is a moving evocation of one individual's discovery of the nature of human dignity, while "Bloodline," exploring the influence of heredity and environment on identity, questions the very concept of race. "The Sky Is Gray," a story that is coming to be considered a classic, presents several different responses to discrimination. One is that of a black preacher who trusts in God to right all wrongs; another is that of his younger, more educated antagonist whose initiation into the ways of the world has turned him into a cynic: "I'm not mad at the world. I'm questioning the world. I'm questioning it with cold logic, sir. What do words like Freedom, Liberty, God, White, Colored mean? I want to know. That's why *you* are sending us to school, to read and to ask questions. And because we ask these questions, you call us mad. No sir, it is not us who are mad." In contrast to these philosophical stances, which are both abrogations of personal responsibility, the young narrator learns from his mother a way of life based on individual integrity and a sense of self-worth.

Gaines, together with other young writers, helped to initiate a new black literary renaissance in the late 1960s and 1970s that was to rival and perhaps exceed in scope and impact the Harlem renaissance of the 1920s. While these newer voices were beginning to be heard, some older voices were still commanding our attention. *Eight Men,* a book of earlier pieces by Richard Wright (1908—1960) appeared in 1961, and in 1963 Langston Hughes (1902—1967) published *Something in Common and Other Stories,* containing a selection of stories from *The Ways of White Folks* (1934) and *Laughing to Keep from Crying* (1952), as well as some previously uncollected works. Whereas Wright's fiction is marked by the use of broad symbolism and characterized by what is sometimes a heavy didacticism, Hughes's is markedly different in style and tone. As a poet who knows the value of conciseness and precision and is well versed in the potential of satire and irony, Hughes manages in his short vignette-like pieces to give full humor and artistic treatment to many of the same major issues raised by Wright.

• • •

The most distinctive voice of the generation between those of Hughes and Gaines is that of James Baldwin (1924—   ). Although Baldwin is primarily a novelist, he has, like Hughes and Wright, demonstrated his ability to work well in several genres, and *Going to Meet the Man* (1965) is a most noteworthy book of short fiction. Two of the stories, "Sonny's Blues" and the title piece, have been widely discussed and anthologized. The former, set in Harlem, celebrates the ability of the individual to discover in art a means of personalizing, expressing, and transcending his own suffering and that of his people: "For, while the tale of how we suffer, and how we are delighted, and how we may triumph is never new, it must always be heard. . . . And this tale, according to that face, that body, those strong hands on those strings, has another aspect in every country, and a new depth in every generation." The latter, set in the South, is one of the most controversial short stories of the postwar period. Going to meet "the man," entering the warped and tormented mind of a Southern sheriff, we discover the effects of his racism not only on the objects of his hatred and violence but also on his own psyche. The story is a chilling testament to the dehumanizing power of bigotry and its capacity for warping reality and turning all parties involved into inhuman grotesques. Carefully crafted and exhibiting a remarkable control of tone and image, "Going to Meet the Man" is evidence that Baldwin, like Gaines and Hughes, is capable of reconciling what he called the "all but irreconcilable war between [the black writer's] social and artistic responsibilities."

•   •   •

The conflict between social and artistic responsibility, or between maintaining a sense of ethnic identity and creating literature of more universal significance, was also successfully resolved by a number of Jewish-American short-story writers in the period following World War II. Literary artists such as Malamud, Bellow, and Singer proved themselves to be most adept at drawing on the linguistic, customary, ethical, and philosophical elements of their cultural backgrounds and at depicting the position of the Jewish-American in society. Although these particular concerns set them apart from the other writers discussed, their interest in examining interpersonal relationships, their skill at developing a sense of place, and their fascination with dream and fantasy place them within the main tradition of American short fiction.

•   •   •

This ability to synthesize traditions is manifest in the works of Brooklyn-born Bernard Malamud (1914—   ). His first volume of short stories, *The Magic Barrel* (1948), won the National Book Award and is regarded by critics as his best and most even collection. Several of the stories take place in Italy; some have non-Jewish protagonists. While these pieces attest to Malamud's range and are far from failures, he is strongest when focusing on the struggles of Jewish protagonists to ensure their economic, social, or spiritual survival in a New York that is part naturalistic wasteland and part fantastic dreamscape.

Malamud's most successful stories depend on the careful maintenance of dynamic tension in both voice and tone: the voice of the Yiddish storyteller, the oral fabulist, framing, breaking through, and playing against realistic description; the serious treatment of serious matters, supported by biblical allusion and patterns of symbols, blended with humor and undercut by irony. In addition, he is often successful dealing with particular and universal themes. Viewed in one light, his New York stories exhibit the naturalist's concern with the impact of environmental and cultural factors on a segment of society. Looked at another way, they are structured by the basic tragic and comic pattern of myth: the individual's quest for identity, his alienation from and reintegration with society.

The first two stories in The Magic Barrel, "The First Seven Years" and "The Mourners," are illustrative. Although there are intervals of impersonal, literary narration in both stories—"The shoemaker shrugged and continued to peer through the partly frosted window at the near-sighted haze of falling snow"—we hear the distinctive voice of the storyteller constantly breaking through, particularly in the inversions of syntax that are characteristic of Yiddish-American dialect: "Who he was the shoemaker for a moment had no idea. . . . " Both voices are often made to serve naturalistic ends, such as demonstrating the dehumanizing effect of urban social and economic deprivation: "In the tenement, although he had lived there ten years, he was more or less unknown. The tenants on both sides of his flat on the fifth floor, an Italian family of three middle-aged sons and their wizened mother, and a sullen childless German couple named Hoffman, never said hello to him, nor did he greet any of them on the way up or down the narrow wooden stairs."

The mythical and biblical allusions in "The First Seven Years" are rendered incongruous by context. Although he possesses a flute, Max is not Mozart's Tamino or even Papageno, but a seedy student, "tall and grotesquely thin, with sharply cut features, particularly a beak-like nose." His birdlike appearance emphasizes not his magical abilities but his mute rapaciousness, and is not mythic amplification but parody. Although Sobel labors seven years for Feld's daughters, the two men are not Jacob and Laban, but poor shoemakers, and the legacy at stake is not Abraham's patrimony but a meager shop that barely provides its owner with a living. "The Mourner" is also marked by contrary patterns of amplification and diminution. Elements of Jewish ritual act to expand the scope of Kessler's mourning; he grieves not only for himself but also for his people and for those who have killed themselves by closing their eyes to suffering. At the same time, however, his lamentation has taken on the quality of obsession, turning him into a grotesque, something less than a complete human being.

Focusing on the particulars of both stories, one can read them as sociology, documents that record and analyze the economic hardships and problems of acculturation that faced the Jewish immigrant. Viewed in this way, the stories, at least initially, present contrasting responses: Feld, desiring a better life for himself and his daughter, buys the American dream of success and social advancement at the cost of other values; Kessler, on the other hand, steadfastly retains his values at the price of isolation and ostracism. To read them solely in this way, however, is to miss another dimension, for both explore in more general terms the roles played by love and suffering in the individual's quest to discover his own identity and his relationships to others.

Still another dimension is added to Malamud's work by his introduction of characters and events that are overtly or faintly supernatural. In "Angel Levine," a tailor named Manischevitz aids and is aided by "an angel from God"; while in "The Magic Barrel," probably Malamud's best story, Leo Finkle, a rabbinical student, is assisted by Salzman, a mysterious marriage broker whose office is "in the air" and who seems at times to be an agent of fate. Yet in Malamud's world, even the supernatural is tainted by the naturalistic, and the sense of wonder generated by seemingly magical transformations or resolutions is undercut by cynicism. Displaying human weakness and a fondness for the pleasures of the flesh, "Angel Levine" is as much in need of help as he is capable of offering it, and Manischevitz discovers him not in some ethereal habitat but in a sleazy Harlem cabaret. Salzman provides Leo with his ideal bride, but she is as much whore as virgin, and his desire for her is as much a product of self-delusion and a need for self-mortification as it is of love.

The fantastic element apparent in these two pieces reappears in two of the stories in Malamud's second collection, *Idiots First* (1963), which many critics consider to be less consistent than *The Magic Barrel*. In the allegorical title story, Mendel struggles to protect the life of his idiot son, fighting time and an antagonist, Ginzburg, who symbolizes death, upholder of the "cosmic universal law," the law of entropy. Mendel's conditional victory over Ginzburg is won through selflessness and compassion, through an assertion of his basic humanity in the face of universal indifference. In "The Jewbird," Harry Cohen is visited by a talking "longbeaked bird" named Schwartz who torments him by exhibiting all of the qualities of the Jewish stereotype. Driven "bats" by the fact that Schwartz is "there always, even in his dreams," Cohen finally attacks the bird and tosses him out onto the sidewalk. Cohen's victory, unlike Mendel's, is delusory, for he has won by stubbornly denying what he is. The fantastic elements in these stories prevent us from reading them as anything but allegory, and our apprehension at the author's seriousness is balanced by his use of humor.

Reprinting the Fidelman stories from the first two volumes and presenting three new ones, *Pictures of Fidelman: An Exhibition* (1969) reveals another Malamud: the literary artist self-consciously examining the difficulties and paradoxes of his vocation. The protagonist of all these pieces is an unsuccessful painter whose situation is summed up by the epigraphs to the volume:

Not to understand. Yes, that was my whole
occupation during those years—I can assure
you, it was not an easy one.
                              R. M. Rilke

            The intellect of man is forced to choose
            Perfection of the life or of the work . . .
                              W. B. Yeats
Both.
                  A. Fidelman

Choosing both, Fidelman continues to botch his life and his art until he is forced to understand that he must accept both on less grandiose terms. Grouped together, Malamud's portraits of the artist cease to be independent short stories, forming instead what the author himself has called a picaresque novel.

Whether he is completely successful or not, Bernard Malamud exhibits in his short fiction an admirable propensity for treating a variety of themes in a variety of manners. A quick glance at some of the stories in his most recent volume, *Rembrandt's Hat* (1973) reveals once again his range and his potential for developing new forms. "The Silver Crown," for instance, is a reexamination of the vagaries of belief, cast in the mold of the earlier fables, while the title story is a more realistic piece which, in its treatment of artistic self-consciousness and failed communication, is in some ways reminiscent of the earlier Fidelman stories. "Talking Horse" is not only different from both of these, but significantly different from anything else Malamud has written. Combining traditional narrative with the kind of question-and-answer format that Joyce employed in *Ulysses* and *Finnegans Wake,* he presents us with a talking horse whose absurd condition ("Am I a man in a horse or a horse that talks like a man?") embodies all of the apparent dualities of human existence.

Looked at as a whole, Malamud's short stories are expressive of the totality of his heritage, of the mystical, ethical, and intellectual impulses that together define the Jewish-American character. This is not to suggest, however, that he is merely a Jewish-American writer. For, as he has indicated: "I handle the Jew as a symbol of the tragic experience of man existentially. I try to see the Jew as universal man. Every man is a Jew though he may not know it" (interview in *Jerusalem Post* [Weekly Overseas Edition], April 1, 1968, p. 13).

• • •

The Jew as universal man preoccupied with existential questions is also a central figure in the fiction of Saul Bellow (1915—   ). Although Bellow was awarded the Nobel Prize in literature primarily on the basis of his novels, his facility with shorter works is demonstrated in *Mosby's Memoirs* (1968), a collection of three short stories from *Seize the Day* plus three newer ones. Like the protagonists of his novels, Bellow's Jews are men who think continuously about themselves and about other men who think. At times, like Rogin in "A Father-To-Be," they may be rescued from the neurotic isolation and cold frustration of their thoughts by a simple act of compassion:

"But there's absolutely nothing wrong with you," she said, and pressed against him from behind, surrounding him, pouring the water gently over him until it seemed to him that the water came from within him, it was the warm fluid of his own secret loving spirit overflowing into the sink, green and foaming, and his anger at his son-to-be disappeared altogether . . .

At other times, as when Dr. Braun contemplates death and the past in "The Old System," the sense of futility that is the product of their tendencies to over-intellectualize may make impossible any emotional rescue from without:

And Dr. Braun, bitterly moved, tried to grasp what emotions were. What good were they! What were they for! And no one wanted them now . . . once humankind had grasped its own idea, that it was human and human through such passions, it began to exploit, to play, to disturb for the sake of exciting disturbance, to make an uproar, a crude circus of feelings. . . . And these tears! When you wept them from the heart, you felt you justified something, understood something. But what did you understand? Again, *nothing*! It was only an intimation of understanding.

Tone is always extremely important in Bellow's fiction, something made clear by the narrator's description of the central consciousness of the title story: "Mr. Mosby—Dr. Mosby really; erudite, maybe even profound; thought much, accomplished much—had made some of the most interesting mistakes a man could make in the twentieth century. He was in Oaxaca now to write his memoirs. He had a grant for the purpose, from the Guggenheim Foundation. And why not?" The irony of this description, really the unconscious irony of self-description, fixes Mosby from the start, directing us in our reading of his "Memoirs." Mosby's "interesting mistakes" (such as displeasing "the institutional gentry" by suggesting "that however deplorable the concentration camps had been, they showed at least the rationality of German political ideas") have made him an exile in Oaxaca where he sits drinking mescal and beer, searching for a way "to put some humor" into his memoirs.

He finds it in the story of Hymen Lustgarten, a Jewish one-time Marxist whose grandiose business plans failed miserably because, "strangely meek, stout, swarthy, kindly," he was hampered further by "a traitorous incompetence." Lustgarten's schemes for stealing a fortune out of the ruins of postwar Europe are deserving of censure. But in using Lustgarten's life story for his own purposes, turning him into a stereotype of bungling failure and greed, Mosby exhibits the intellectual detachment that led to that destruction in the first place. "Having disposed of all things human," exiled himself to the rarefied atmosphere of his own thoughts, he ends up gasping for air like those other victims of twentieth-century rationalism, the Jews of Auschwitz and Dachau.

•   •   •

Whereas Bellow's characters endlessly cogitate on what it means to be human, the Jews we encounter in Philip Roth's *Goodbye, Columbus and Five Short Stories* (1959) are preoccupied with what it means to be Jewish. Neil Klugman's confrontation with the world of American-Jewish aristocracy in the novella *Goodbye, Columbus* is a rite of passage with which many readers and moviegoers are quite familiar. Three of Roth's short stories, however, present differing versions of the process of self-discovery.

In "The Conversion of the Jews," a pesty young student, annoying because he asks the wrong questions, forces his hypocritical elders to break through the walls of stale dogma and intolerance and admit what should be considered truths by Jew and Christian alike, that "God can do Anything" and that "You should never hit anybody about God." In "Defender of the Faith," Sergeant Nathan Marx must see through another kind of hypocrisy, that of an army recruit who plays on Nathan's sense of kinship, using his Jewishness as an excuse for escaping duties and gaining favors. While Ozzie Freedman recovers the basic religious tenets of his culture by pretending to become a Christian savior, Nathan Marx discovers its ethical basis by rejecting a certain type of Jew. Finally, in "Eli, the Fanatic," a practical suburban lawyer changes clothes with a religious fanatic and reclaims the lost consciousness of suffering that is a part of his heritage, saving himself from the pretenses of his shallow community and becoming a madman in the eyes of his neighbors and family.

Although in all of these stories Roth teaches us important lessons about ethnic and individual identity, he avoids didacticism by employing his excellent comic skills, demonstrating why *Goodbye, Columbus* won a National Book Award.

•   •   •

The voices of Malamud, Bellow, and Roth were, of course, not the only Jewish-American voices to be heard in the short fiction of the period. Grace Paley's (1922—   ) first volume of stories, *The Little Disturbances of Man,* published in 1959 and reissued in 1968, exhibited for the first time to a large audience her unique treatment of description and dialogue. In "The Loudest Voice," for example, she evokes a sense of the past by focusing on the sounds of childhood: "There is a certain place where dumb-waiters boom, doors slam, dishes crash; every window is a mother's mouth bidding the street shut up, go skate somewhere else, come home. My voice is the loudest."

Elsewhere, as in "Goodbye and Good Luck," a tale of love lost and regained in the Yiddish theater, she is very adept at capturing the rhythms and diction of Jewish-American dialect:

I was popular in certain circles, says Aunt Rose. I wasn't no thinner then, only more stationary in the flesh. In time to come, Lillie, don't be surprised—change is a fact of God. From this no one is excused. Only a person like your mama stands on one foot, she don't notice how big her behind is getting and sings in the canary's ear for thirty years. Who's listening?

• • •

Herbert Gold (1929—   ) explored love, isolation, and responsibility, in his collection *Love and Like* (1960), and 1965 saw the appearance of a noteworthy first collection by Hugh Nissenson, *A Pile of Stories.* In the same year, Stanley Elkin published *Criers and Kibitzers, Kibitzers and Criers,* the title story of which employs Jewish folk philosophy to demonstrate the emotional and ethical blindness that results from reducing complex human matters to facile formulations.

• • •

One of the most distinctive writers of the period, however, is Isaac Bashevis Singer (1909—   ). Singer is something of an anomaly. Amazingly prolific, he has nonetheless proved himself consistently excellent, winning a National Book Award in 1973 and the Nobel Prize for Literature in 1978. A Polish Jew who has lived in the United States since 1935, he has continued to write in Yiddish, often assisting in the subsequent translation of his work into English. Describing his method in the Author's Note to *An Isaac Bashevis Singer Reader* (1971), he points out, "Because of this, I can call myself a bilingual writer and say that English has become my 'second original.'"

In the late 1950s to late 1960s Singer published four volumes of short stories—*Gimpel the Fool* (1957), *The Spinoza of Market Street* (1961), *Short Friday* (1964), and *The Seance* (1968)—and several illustrated books of stories for children. The latter are remarkable in their similarity to his tales for adults, manifesting the same concern with the supernatural and taking place in the same wonderful world in which the past survives, coloring and informing our sense of the present. As Singer notes in the Foreword to *Zlateh the Goat* (1966):

Children are as puzzled by passing time as grownups. What happens to a day once it is gone? Where are all our yesterdays with their joys and sorrows? Literature helps us remember the past with its many moods. To the story-teller yesterday is still here as are the years and decades gone by. In stories time does not vanish. Neither do men and animals. For the writer and his reader all creatures go on living forever. What happened long ago is still present.

The majority of Singer's stories are set in the recreated past, in the late nineteenth-century and early twentieth-century hamlets and cities of his native Poland, in Frampol, Chelm, Lublin, and Warsaw. It is a past recaptured not only through recording the physical details of landscape, dress, and daily activity, but also through evoking the mood of the people who inhabited it, as embodied in their philosophy, their customs, and their rituals. Defined in this way, mood becomes more important to Singer than character and setting—or, rather, mood becomes character and setting. Even Singer's contemporary Jewish-Americans, residing in New York and Florida, share to a large extent the same sense of reality that shapes and informs the lives of Gimpel, Zlateh, or The Spinoza of Market Street.

The view of reality that they share is a product of their cultural heritage and of the memory, dreams, and imagination of the storyteller. What Gimpel says of himself could also be applied to his creator:

I heard a great deal, many lies and falsehoods, but the longer I lived the more I understood that there were really no lies. Whatever doesn't really happen is dreamed at night. It happens to one if it doesn't happen to another, tomorrow if not today, or a century hence if not next year. What difference can it make? Often I heard tales of which I said, "Now this is a thing that cannot happen." But before a year had elapsed I heard that it actually had come to pass somewhere.

Going from place to place, eating at strange tables, it often happens that I spin yarns—improbable things that could never have happened—about devils, magicians, windmills and the like.

Singer's stories are filled with improbable events—mysterious transformations, occurrences that defy the principle of causality—and populated with human grotesques and supernatural beings, dwarfs, giants, crones, imps, devils, and angels.

The voice of the storyteller, heard through impersonal narrative or speaking through the voices of his various personas, entrances us. Once captivated, taking things on his terms, we are subject to his remarkable skill at depicting full, human characters. Discovering human qualities in even the most strange and fantastic creatures, we end up by willingly suspending our disbelief to the point of accepting the entirety of Singer's bizarre universe.

Singer does more than convince us to suspend our sense of reality; he questions it. At the conclusion of "Gimpel the Fool," Gimpel notes, "No doubt the world is entirely an imaginary world, but it is only once removed from the true world. At the door of the hovel where I lie, there stands the plank on which the dead are taken away. . . . When the time comes I will go joyfully. Whatever may be there, it will be real, without complication, without ridicule, without deception." Although the storyteller's universe is admittedly a fiction, so too, he indicates, is ours. "What difference does it make?" Gimpel asks us. What real difference is there, Singer seems to suggest, between viewing ourselves as creatures composed of id and superego or as creatures controlled by devils and angels, between conceiving of the cosmos as patterns of waves, forms of energy, or as a thought in the mind of God?

This is not to say that Singer considers human actions to be meaningless. While he almost never moralizes, he is a moralist, and his stories are intended to serve, at least partially, as instruction. At first glance, however, it may be difficult for us to determine exactly what it is that we are expected to learn from the stories, for they appear to present us with a world characterized as much by injustice as justice, one in which good and evil are equally powerful forces, and in which men are both governed by fate and possessed of free will.

In a story such as "The Gentleman from Cracow," for example, we get what we expect. The people of Frampol, succumbing to their passion for gold, place themselves in the hands of a stranger, in reality Ketev Mriri, Chief of the Devils. As a result, everything is turned topsy-turvy, demons dance in the streets, all the first-born of the village die, and the townspeople become perpetual paupers, preserving always a hatred of wealth. The moral here seems clear. But what are we to make of "Under the Knife," in which Leib rewards a prostitute's kindness by killing her, or "Fire," in which a man is assumed to be guilty of a crime he only imagined committing? What of Singer's dwarfs, cripples, witches, and fools, condemned to be what they are by accidents of birth or the perceptions of others?

The answer lies, again, in recognizing our limitations. "The world is full of puzzles," Singer tells us. "It is possible that not even Elijah will be able to answer all our questions when the Messiah comes." Although the results of our actions in this world may seem contradictory, although we may see kindness punished and cruelty rewarded, our choices do, ultimately, matter. For, as one of Singer's characters puts it: "There is a God. There is a purpose in creation. Copulation, free will, fate—all are part of His plan." Not knowing the plan and being unable to judge our own deeds solely on the basis of the fruits they bear, we must rely on something like common sense, our intuition of what is proper and natural.

In "Big and Little," a man who has been ridiculed during his entire life for his smallness forces his wife to marry a giant when he himself dies. After describing the disastrous consequences, the storyteller comments: "As I was saying—spite. . . . One shouldn't tease. Little is little, and big is big. It's not our world. We didn't make it. But for a man to do such an unnatural thing! Did you ever hear the like of it? Surely the evil one must have gotten into him. I shudder every time I think of it."

• • •

It may initially seem extremely capricious to compare the short fiction of Singer, a Polish Jew, with that of Flannery O'Connor (1925—1964), a Southern Catholic. Certainly, the particulars of time and place and the cultural backgrounds on which they draw are quite different, as are their narrative techniques. Moreover, whereas there are often overt supernatural elements in Singer's stories, O'Connor's fiction is always firmly rooted in the physical. Yet there are similarities that balance out the differences. Like Singer, O'Connor is deeply concerned with ethical questions but never didactic or moralistic, and her work, like his, often focuses on human limitation and deformity.

O'Connor's second, and last, volume of short stories, *Everything that Rises must Converge* (1965), exhibits once again her preoccupation with the grotesque, with individuals who are physical, emotional, mental, and spiritual cripples. Unlike writers such as John Cheever, who may discover the bizarre in the usual, Flannery O'Connor is an artist for whom the everyday *is* bizarre. In a lecture at Notre Dame University (quoted in the Introduction to *Everything that Rises must Converge*), she noted: "I doubt if the texture of Southern life is any more grotesque than that of the rest of the nation, but it does seem evident that the Southern writer is particularly adept at recogniz- ing the grotesque; and to recognize the grotesque, you have to have some notion of what is not grotesque and why . . ." It is this awareness, this acuity of vision, that permits her to turn the description of a doctor's office in "Revelation" into a catalogue of distortion and ugliness:

Next to her was a fat girl of eighteen or nineteen, scowling into a thick blue book which Mrs. Turpin saw was entitled *Human Development*. The girl raised her head and directed her scowl at Mrs. Turpin as if she did not like her looks. She appeared annoyed that anyone should speak while she tried to read. The poor girl's face was blue with acne and Mrs. Turpin thought how pitiful it was to have a face like that at that age. . . . Next to the ugly girl was the child, still in exactly the same position, and next to him was a thin leathery old woman in a cotton print dress. She and Claud had three sacks of chicken food in their pumphouses that was in the same print. . . . And at right angles but next to the well-dressed pleasant lady was a lank-faced woman who was certainly the child's mother. She had on a yellow sweat shirt and wine-colored slacks, both gritty-looking, and the rims of her lips were stained with snuff. Her dirty yellow hair was tied behind with a little piece of red paper ribbon.

There are difficulties with reading symbolic content into any of O'Connor's descriptions, for things usually become symbols only when her characters see them as such. This description, however, coming in one of her best stories, may be viewed as something close to a metaphor for the world of her fiction in which all are ill, all are patients awaiting cure. Their sickness lies not only in the fact that they are spiritual beings trapped within physical prisons, but also in the fact that, although obviously limited, they presume completely to understand that condition and the means by which they may transcend it. Thinking that she is better and different, Mrs. Turpin is just as deformed as the acne-scarred young girl, and in the girl's eyes, just as ugly, just as much a parody of human development.

As many critics have noticed, the title of O'Connor's second collection is taken from Teilhard de Chardin, the French Jesuit who viewed human evolution as a teleologic physical and spiritual process. Looked at in the light of her comment that the book contains "nine stories about original sin," her choice of title must be viewed as at least partially ironic, which is borne out by careful reading of the stories.

Indeed, in O'Connor's universe man is not Teilhard's totally unique being, evolving in time toward physical and spiritual perfection, but a limited creature incapable of completely comprehending the mechanism of salvation and embodying two aspects of the Fall: the descent into flawed physicality that resulted from it and the sinful pride that led to it.

Focusing purely on the physical, O'Connor's characters find that they and others are not products of Teilhard's separate human line of development, but very much members of the animal kingdom. Parker's ugly wife is "a giant hawk-eyed angel" with "a terrible bristly claw" ("Parker's Back"). Tanner, we are told, "had looked like a monkey" when he was young, "but when he got old, he looked like a bear" ("Judgement Day"). Having been called "a wart hog from hell" by the blue-faced young girl, Ruby Turpin, her own face turned greenish blue from a bruise, stands confused before her "pig parlor": "How am I a hog and me both? How am I saved and from hell too?"

Just as the physical condition of O'Connor's characters belies Teilhard's notion of developing perfection in the "biosphere," so too does their social interaction contradict his notion of positive evolution in the "nousphere."

Most of the pieces in this volume present twisted relationships between parents and children. Julian sees his mother only as an ignorant and ridiculous bigot and toys with "ways by which he could teach her a lesson" ("Everything that Rises must Converge"). Asbury, a similar character, looks on his mother as a literal-minded fool whose sole purpose is to suffocate him ("The Enduring Chill"). Thomas, feeling helpless before his mother, acts on the perverted concept of manhood that is his father's legacy to him ("The Comforts of Home"). If this represents continuity between generations, if this is the quality of inheritance, what are we to think of the concept of spiritual evolution? Where are we to find the human difference?

One place we clearly cannot find it is in any human rational faculty. It is when O'Connor's characters feel they have things figured out that they are most in trouble. Believing that he knows how to appease his wife, Parker has a portrait of Christ tattooed on his back, only to have her accuse him of idolatry and attack him with a broom ("Parker's Back"). Relying on his notion of psychology, Sheppard (another version of Rayber in her novel, *The Violent Bear it Away*) attempts to rehabilitate a lame juvenile delinquent ("The Lame Shall Enter First"). Not only does he fail to change the boy, who ends up making a fool of him, he fails to understand and love his own son, who ends up committing suicide.

Is there, then, a solution to Mrs. Turpin's dilemma: "How am I a hog and me both? How am I saved and from hell too?" For O'Connor, the answer seems to be that as imperfect creatures we are like animals, condemned to physicality, suffering, and ignorance. Yet we are different because we may ultimately be saved. Looking up to heaven at the end of "Revelation," Mrs. Turpin sees

> . . . a vast swinging bridge extending upward from the earth through a field of living fire. Upon it a vast horde of souls were fumbling toward heaven. There were whole companies of white-trash, clean for the first time in their lives, and bands of black niggers in white robes, and battalions of freaks and lunatics shouting and clapping and leaping like frogs. And bringing up the procession was a tribe of people whom she recognized at once as those who, like herself and Claud, had always had a little of everything and the God-given wit to use it right. They were marching behind the others with great dignity, accountable as they had always been for good order and common sense and respectable behavior. They alone were on key. Yet she could see by their shocked and altered faces that even their virtues were being burned away.

We are different, but to assert this difference or to attempt fully to comprehend it is to lose sight of it. To O'Connor the prideful person and the self-proclaimed prophet both suffer from blindness, for the one fails to see that all are equal in purgation, and the other pretends to see something beyond our perception.

In another statement reprinted in the Introduction to *Everything that Rises must Converge,* she says, "The serious fiction writer will think that any story that can be entirely explained by the adequate motivation of the characters or by a believable imitation of a way of life or by a proper theology, will not be a large enough story for him to occupy himself with. . . . The fiction writer presents mystery through manners, grace through nature, but when he finishes, there always has to be left over that sense of Mystery which cannot be accounted for by any human formula." Everything that rises must converge, but for O'Connor as for Singer, not necessarily in this world or in a manner we can ever understand.

*   *   *

O'Connor's sense of the usual as bizarre is shared by James Purdy (1923—   ). In *Color of Darkness* (1957) and *Children Is All* (1962), he creates characters who are marked by physical deformities and behavioral aberrations, victims of indefinite horrors and compulsions. Trapped within themselves, his people seek absurdly futile ways out. One tries to assert his identity by shaving his beard ("The Cutting Edge"); another attempts to alter hers by refusing to be called by her married name ("Don't Call Me by My Right Name"). Most often, what we see are people mechanically performing meaningless rituals, and as the title of one of his stories indicates, what we almost always hear is nothing but the "Sound of Talking." Unlike Singer and O'Connor, Purdy does not even suggest that there may be a purpose to what he sees as the absurd condition of contemporary society, nor does he offer any hope for his human grotesques. As the protagonist of one of his disturbing modern horror stories puts it: "There isn't anything to say about such private sorrow. You just wait till the lights go out and then reach for your hat" ("You Reach for Your Hat" in *Color of Darkness*).

*   *   *

There are, of course, possible responses to the absurdity and surrealism of contemporary existence other than to suggest that such things are aspects of man's fallen condition or that they simply are. One such response is to consider progress and technology as possible contributors to alienation and dehumanization. Since the time of H. G. Wells, examination of this causal relationship has served as subject matter of works by the best practitioners of science fiction. Living in the age of Sputnik and in the shadow of the bomb, a number of competent short-story writers in the late 1950s and early 1960s chose to work with this fictional form (which has its roots in romance), contributing pieces to the plethora of science fiction publications that arose in the period, and which increased the respectability of the genre. Although Kurt Vonnegut (1922—   ), for example, is now considered a mainstream, if experimental, author, he began by writing short stories that must be classified as science fiction, exploring in *Welcome to the Monkey House* (1968) the possible effects of technological advances on ethics, politics, and human sexuality. A similar concern with the implications of scientific progress characterizes the work of Ray Bradbury (1920—   ), a science fiction writer who has exhibited an admirable degree of literary artistry in several fine volumes of stories in the period: *A Medicine for Melancholy* (1959), *The Machineries of Joy* (1964), *The Vintage Bradbury* (1965), *The Autumn People* (1965), and *Tomorrow Midnight* (1966).

• • •

Another possible response to absurdity, one very much evident in O'Connor's work, is to emphasize the contradictory and the mechanical through humor. Confronted with what is obviously absurd and irreconcilable, the contemporary writer may find that the only justifiable reaction is laughter in the dark. So intrinsic is this attitude to the twentieth-century American zeitgeist that it has given rise to a tradition of black humor that is seen in the novels of Nathanael West, Joseph Heller, and Thomas Pynchon, and the short stories of Jean Stafford (1915—1979) and Bruce J. Friedman (1930—   ).

Several of the pieces in Stafford's second collection, *Bad Characters* (1964), are anything but humorous. "Cops and Robbers" is a chilling portrait of parental cruelty, while "A Winter's Tale" is a subdued but relentless story in which Stafford carefully draws a character sketch that not only exposes one individual's capacity for evil, but evokes the Evil unleashed in Germany in the 1930s and 1940s. Most of the other pieces, however, range in tone from the bizarrely comic to bitingly ironic. Whether she is using a child protagonist to mock the doctrine of alienation ("Bad Characters"), satirizing the modern cult of youth and beauty ("The End of a Career"), or dissecting the academic mentality ("Caveat Emptor"), Stafford creates a universe that is at once absurdly ludicrous and convincingly real. As the Author's Note to the collection makes clear, her world is populated by characters who are either victims or possessed of "wicked hearts." Encountering this rogue's gallery and finding our own portraits there, we have no recourse but self-consciously to laugh.

Friedman's sense of humor is even more outre and in its extravagance, even more characteristic of the black humor of the 1950s and 1960s. In *Far from the City of Class* (1963) and *Black Angels* (1966), he not only wickedly satirizes many facets of contemporary culture—our commercialism and media addiction, our fascination with psychoanalysis, our growing inurement to death and violence—he mocks our willingness to believe and our gullibility as readers. "Yes, We Have No Ritchard" burlesques the banality and ludicrousness of the traditional concept of heaven, ridiculing as well our need to believe in an abstract system of rewards and punishments that will ultimately determine our worth. "The Mission" is nothing more than a shaggy dog story that plays on the reader's desire to discover significance, and "The Night Boxing Ended" is really an extended joke at the reader's expense. In a mock-serious tone, Friedman realistically describes a dull prizefight, sets us up by depicting the reactions of the crowd, recording one of the spectator's cries for more violence, and delivers the punchline: one of the fighters *does* knock the other's head off, and it floats out over the arena.

• • •

This kind of play, based on the assumption that writer and reader are engaged in a contest of wits, is also typical of the fiction of Vladimir Nabokov (1899—1977), the Russian-born novelist, poet, playwright, translator, and short-story writer. As Page Stegner notes in the introduction to *Nabokov's Congeries* (1968), referring to one of Nabokov's favorite analogies:

Certainly one of the most characteristic aspects of Nabokov's art is the composition of riddles, word games, sleights of hand, false bottoms that drop out from under a reader like the trap door in a gallows. . . . The contest in chess, he says, is between the composer and his hypothetical solver, just as in fiction the contest is between the author and his reader, and the value of a problem lies in the number of "'tries'—delusive opening moves, false scents, specious lines of play, astutely and lovingly prepared to lead the would-be solver astray." The author establishes certain rules to which he adheres, creates barriers which he tries to hurdle, takes the most devious and difficult route from point A to point B, and invites the reader to follow.

Most of the collections which were published by Nabokov in the period or issued after his death consist of stories that first appeared much earlier or were English translations of earlier Russian stories. Although his work therefore does not strictly speaking lie within the province of this study, it is worthy of mention because of its influence on and similarity to the innovationist literature of the 1960s. In his adoption of the role of a conjurer who exposes his tricks, and in his love of parody, puns, mazes, and mirrors, he anticipated the later work of writers such as Barthelme and Barth.

The "Vane Sisters" from *Nabokov's Quartet,* one of the few entirely new stories Nabokov wrote during the period, is an excellent case in point. The narrator, a professor of French literature at a small girls' college, begins by describing the day on which he heard of Cynthia Vane's death, a day of glittering icicles and surreal parking meters:

And as I looked up at the eaves of the adjacent garage with its full display of transparent stalactites backed by their blue silhouettes, I was rewarded at last, upon choosing one, by the sight of what might be described as the dot of an exclamation mark leaving its ordinary position to glide down very fast—a jot faster than the thaw-drop it raced. . . . The lean ghost, the elongated umbra cast by a parking meter upon some damp snow, had a strange ruddy tinge. . . .

Contemplating the parking meter, the narrator runs across D., who informs him of Cynthia's death, and we plunge into a series of reminiscences of the two sisters: Sybil, who had committed suicide months before, and Cynthia, a spiritualist who had professed to be in contact with her dead sister.

Following Cynthia's own death, the narrator discovers that his attitude has changed, that he no longer finds Cynthia's "ridiculous fondness for spiritualism" to be another of her "ingenious fancies." He begins to detect her spiritual presence everywhere and, as the final paragraph indicates, is obsessed by the notion that she has sent him a message that he cannot decipher: "I could isolate, consciously, little. Everything seemed blurred, yellow-clouded, yielding nothing tangible. Her inept acrostics, maudlin evasions, theopathies—every recollection formed ripples of mysterious meaning. Everything seemed yellowly blurred, illusive, lost." The reader who is alert to Nabokov's own evasions will have discovered earlier the key to this last paragraph: "And I wish I could recollect that novel or short story (by some contemporary writer, I believe) in which, unknown to its author, the first letters of the words in its last paragraph formed, as deciphered by Cynthia, a message from his dead mother."

Containing such a mysterious acrostic, the ultimate paragraph of "The Vane Sisters" causes us to doubt the fictional principles of verisimilitude and narrative integrity. If the narrator is unaware of the message, who has composed it?—the Vane sisters; or a godlike author who is toying with his reader, testing his powers of recall and observation? It also calls into question our tacit acceptance of the notion that art is derived from experience and that it comments on it in some significant way. Playing Nabokov's game, we may ask ourselves the same question posed in the verse by Frederic Meyers, which is quoted in the story:

What is this—a conjuror's rabbit,
Or a flawy but genuine gleam—
Which can check the perilous habit
And dispel the dolorous dream?

• • •

The propensity for game playing and tendency toward parody apparent in most of Nabokov's work are also evident in other short fiction of the period. Many of Shirley Jackson's short stories, collected in *The Magic of Shirley Jackson* (1966), take place in a fictional universe that appears to be governed by its own physical laws and its own logic. The title story of George P. Elliott's *Among the Dangs* also plays on our expectation of truth by presenting us with a narrative that is similar to the autobiographical anthropology of a writer such as Margaret Mead, and with a narrator who comes to believe in the role he has adopted to carry out his studies.

· · ·

The most thorough and innovative manipulation and exposure of literary convention in the period, however, is to be found in *Lost in the Funhouse* (1968) by John Barth (1930—   ). The first piece in the volume, "Frame-Tale," is an emblem of the whole. It consists of a strip of paper, which is to be cut out, twisted, and fastened end to end, and which reads "ONCE UPON A TIME THERE WAS A STORY THAT BEGAN." "Frame Tale," like *Lost in the Funhouse* itself, is a Möbius strip that appears to be three-dimensional but is in actuality a two-dimensional, single surface that twists in on itself endlessly. Like an imaginary traveler on such a strip, the reader of Barth's book may for a time be deceived by the illusion of progress or development, only to discover that he has returned to where he began. Lost in the funhouse of fiction or of any other conceptual model of the universe, the reader has his desire for significance repeatedly frustrated on a number of different levels.

Persisting in the belief that the "senselessest babble, could we ken it, might disclose a dark message, or prayer" ("Glossolalia"), the reader who has been trained to search the text for clues will find a profusion of them here. Several of the pieces, for example, are filled with freudian symbolism, sexual puns, and oedipal relationships. Others treat mythological subjects or invoke mythic parallels, and the sequence as a whole follows the pattern of heroic quest described by Lord Raglan and Joseph Campbell.

Like Nabokov, however, Barth makes a farce of freudianism. His use of language that is psychosexually charged is gross, cliched, obvious, and ludicrous, a joke at the expense of both the assumed author of his pieces and the reader who may feel that he has discovered the meaning of his heavy-handed symbolism. The mythic parallels are similarly farcical—Barth's artist-hero becomes bogged down in language, in the manner of telling his tale, and his quest for self-expression concludes, like Tristram Shandy's, with much "left unsaid, much" which "must be blank."

The reader who puts aside any desire for significance, settling for plot and character development, will be equally frustrated. "Lost in the Funhouse," for instance, makes intermittent reference to the conventional pattern of narrative development and to its own inability to follow it: "A long time ago we should have passed the apex of Freitag's Triangle and made brief work of the *denouement;* the plot doesn't rise by meaningful steps but winds upon itself, digresses, retreats, hesitates, sighs, collapses, expires. The climax of the story must be its protagonist's discovery of a way to get through the funhouse. But he has found none, may have ceased to search."

In another piece, "Menelaiad," Barth creates a mirror-maze such as Borges might devise, a structure of tales within tales that thrusts the reader into a state of confusion in which it is impossible with certainty to determine who is saying what:

"""""'Why?' I repeated," I repeated,' I repeated," I repeated,' I repeated," I repeat.
"""""'And the woman, with a bride-shy smile and hushed voice, replied: 'Why what?'

The narrator of "Life-Story," which purports to be autobiography, discovers that he is "in a sense his own author, telling his story to himself." The main "character" of "Autobiography," we are told, is a monophonic recorded authorial voice that calls itself "a fiction without real hope," a "halt narrative: first person, tiresome." If we cannot read for plot, characterization, or extra-textual significance, "for what discreditable motive" ("Life-Story") do we go on?

We continue to read because, while denying our conventional expectations, Barth manages to satisfy our hunger for language and to create intricate and often pleasing literary artifacts. As he himself noted:

Contemporary writers can't go on doing what's been done, and done better. I revere Flaubert and Tolstoy, Hemingway and Faulkner; but they're finished as objects of interest to the writer. My God, we're living in the last third of the twentieth century. We can't write nineteenth-century novels ... Beckett is moving toward silence, refining language out of existence, working toward the point where there's nothing more to say. And Borges writes as if literature had already been done and he's writing footnotes to imaginary texts.

But my temperament is entirely different . . . I start with the premise of the "end of literature" and try to turn it against itself. I go back to Cervantes, Fielding, Sterne, the *Arabian Nights,* to the artificial frame and the long connected tales. I'm interested in the *artifices* of narrative, in what can be done with language.

For Barth, language and literature are both meaningless and ultimately significant. As products of the mind, they are obviously artificial; as the intrinsic forms of human perception and understanding, they may be all we have.

•   •   •

The self-conscious artificiality of *Lost in the Funhouse* was to prove characteristic of one kind of short fiction written in the late 1960s and the 1970s—the experimental stories of Donald Barthelme, Joyce Carol Oates, and others. Barth's refusal to play the Jamesian game was not reflective, however, of a universal attitude toward the genre. For in the subsequent decade many short-story writers continued to rely on the traditional elements of narration, description, plot, dialogue, and characterization.

E. P. Walkiewicz

Oklahoma State University

1969—1980:
EXPERIMENT AND
TRADITION

Short fiction of the 1960s and 1970s was heavily influenced by the intellectual turbulence caused by such forces as the civil-rights movement and the Vietnam conflict. The amount of experimental work being written increased markedly during this era, and once the styles became better defined, a debate developed between traditionalists and experimentalists.

Traditional fiction proceeds on premises solidified with the rise of the novel in the eighteenth century: there is objective reality, and the best way to involve the reader's thoughts and feelings is to use convincing characters in believable situations. The experimental style grew from the belief that post-World War II civilization had undergone such radical changes that old forms no longer met new needs of expression. In their writing, experimentalists question the existence of objective reality. Although the possible forms of experimentation are by definition unlimited, the most common ones are metafiction (as in Curley's "Who, What, Where, When—Why?") surrealism, and discontinuous narrative (as in Barthelme's "Views of My Father Weeping").

Although the stories cited herein occasionally mention civil rights and the war, the effects of those times reach much deeper into the outlook of a writer than merely into subject matter. The world view of the individual writer shapes style and makes a philosophical statement, however muted it may be, and the frame of reference within which characters are placed determines the focus of the work. Writers are discussed here in the context of themes that they use most frequently (or most successfully) to establish the identity of their characters: society at large, ethnic or religious group, or the family. Of course, no writer fits exclusively into one category, but this format will serve as a foundation for the study.

Characters who are presented primarily in relation to the mass of society, and not in relation to a smaller group within it, are inevitably and severely alienated. Either they utterly reject their family or ethnic ties, or struggle with shifting contexts. They tend to relate to society as a whole, although they may find solace in temporary romances. Typical examples are stories by Donald Barthelme, Ann Beattie, Doris Betts, Ray Bradbury, Herbert Gold, Shirley Ann Grau, James B. Hall, Joyce Carol Oates, and Irwin Shaw.

There is also a logical extension of these alienated characters: outcasts. They are defined by the society in which they live, but to which, in fact, they do not belong. Some are outcasts because their vision places them beyond the limits of one society and into history itself. Such characters dominate the stories of Guy Davenport and appear in some by Russell Banks. Others are foreigners or pariahs, as is usually the case with characters in stories by Paul Bowles, H.E. Francis, and Paul Theroux. The styles of these writers are diverse.

A more personal context than society is the ethnic or religious group. The struggles of characters who are caught inside these more confining limits (social, racial, or religious) are often more intense than those of people standing up to society at large. Along with more violent conflict, however, comes greater hope that their actions will make a difference, since the arenas of personal battles are smaller. Louis Auchincloss, James Alan McPherson, Leonard Michaels, Hugh Nissenson, Flannery O'Connor, J. F. Powers, and I. B. Singer fill their stories with the cadence and vocabulary of the social groups of which they write.

The most intimate context of anybody's identity is the family—the easiest to recognize and the hardest to escape. The closeness of family members offers countless opportunities for writers to portray dramatic conflicts that exemplify basic human problems. People feel alienated from each other in any of the three contexts mentioned, but alienation within the society is the most bewildering, while within the family it is the most painful. Regardless of this, however, the family is the most consistent source of consolation in American short stories of the 1960s and 1970s. Writers relying primarily on family matters are Frederick Busch, Raymond Carver, Daniel Curley, Grace Paley, Richard Stern, Barry Targan, Peter Taylor, and John Updike.

Looking at such writers in terms of the broad scope of their fiction reveals a sense of similar purposes and shows some parallels of style and theme.

•   •   •

From the prominence of The New Yorker, Donald Barthelme (1931—   ) exerted a formidable influence on the short story of the two decades. Of recent writers of short experimental works (such as John Barth, Robert Coover, and Ronald Sukenick), Barthelme has had the most visible and enduring impact on American fiction.

A virtue he shares with most successful experimental writers is a piercing eye for the absurdities of conventional behavior, an awareness that seems to have been the starting point for most experimentalists. He has a fine ear for language and can make trenchant social criticism by his use of idiom and vernacular.

Barthelme's stories can be classified according to clarity: the obscure stories ("The Piano Player," "Views of My Father Weeping," and "City Life"), which are amusing, coherent, subtle, and clear; and the didactic stories ("A Shower of Gold," "The Glass Mountain," and "Kierkegaard Unfair to Schlegel"), which proclaim theme at the expense of subtlety. These classifications that straddle either side of the so-called balanced story contain difficulties that often trip writers of new fiction. Experimentalists tend to reduce coherent action and depth of character in favor of manipulating form and word-play. When they fail, they can either land in the hole of meaningless obscurity or in the safety net of flat didactic statements.

Come Back, Dr. Caligari (1964) contains stories that contributed substantially to Barthelme's reputation, and are representative of tales found throughout the body of his work. "The Piano Player" presents much of what Barthelme's critics have attacked: deteriorating absurd conversation, repeated incantation of a key term ("ugliness" in this case), incongruous and incoherent action, and a chaotic conclusion (the daughter's piano strikes the father dead). The story is fragmented and strained by clashes of images and ideas.

Quite different from the obscure stories is "A Shower of Gold," in which the sculptor Peterson conducts a TV talk show that the producers have determined should be a platform for expressing twentieth-century alienation. After playing along for a while, he rebels and announces his credo to the audience: "In this kind of world . . . absurd if you will . . . there are opportunities for beginning again . . . How can you be alienated without first having been connected?"

Balanced stories, such as "Me and Miss Mandible" and "Marie, Marie, Hold on Tight," find the middle ground and effectively combine incongruity and commitment to theme. The first appears as the diary entries of a thirty-five-year-old who has been unaccountably put back into the sixth grade. The story points out the arbitrariness of social convention and the necessity of conformity as the narrator learns that he must "pick up the clues" to prosper in a baffling society. The second story tells the agony of three men who "demonstrate against the human condition" by picketing a church, asking, "Why does it have to be this way?" After they are beaten by thugs, one returns and delivers a speech the next night. The narrator explains, "He was very eloquent. And Eloquence, Henry Mackie says, is really all any of us can hope for." In this allegory of the modern writer performing his role, human warmth conveys humor and makes a resonant statement.

City Life (1970) is generally a weaker collection than *Caligari*. "The Tolstoy Museum" and "Brain Damage" are presented through words and illustrations, and they achieve an occasional sharp stroke of satire. "The Glass Mountain," a didactic first-person-absurd story of a man scaling a skyscraper, appears in the form of one hundred brief entries (mostly single sentences) that are the allegory of a romantic hero's quest for excellence in a corrupt society. "City Life" is the story of two young women suffering various hardships of involvement in society, deciding that they dislike city life, but surrendering to it at last. The final despair is clear. "Views of My Father Weeping" is told by a bewildered first-person narrator, and the story is obscured by a montage of incongruous elements: a mixture of nineteenth-century and twentieth-century images and motifs from cowboy movies and freudian psychology. By contrast, the meaning of "Kierkegaard Unfair to Schlegel" is clear because it is a philosophical discourse rather than a conventional story. The reader is finally led to believe that irony is not satisfying, but it is acceptable, rather like the eloquence mentioned in "Marie, Marie, Hold on Tight." Here there is less of the dramatic texture of the earlier story.

As such stories illustrate, Barthelme tends to use either the coldly objective third-person narrator or the bewildered first person. Both techniques keep the reader at a distance from the characters and, to use Wayne C. Booth's term from *The Rhetoric of Fiction,* at a distance from the "implied author." When the author strikes an indifferent pose toward his characters, it is hard for the reader to care about them.

"Daumier," from *Sadness* (1972), is one of Barthelme's finest stories, complex but ultimately rewarding. Daumier complains of his "hankering" and "rapacious" feelings. He proposes to compensate for his imbalance by creating a world in which everyone's flaws are balanced out by his surrogate form. This world is made of Western-movie characters and plot devices. The counterpart of Daumier's real-life Amelia is Celeste (a parody of a Corinne Calvet character from a Western about mail-order brides), who is voluptuous and speaks in broken English and French. A narrative voice describes her:

> Then Daumier looked at Celeste and saw that the legs on her were as long and slim as his hope of Heaven and the thighs on her were as strong and sweet-shaped as ampersands and the buttocks on her were as pretty as two pictures and the waist on her was as neat and in-curved as a fiddle and the shoulders on her were as tempting as sex crimes and the hair on her was as long and black as Lent and the movement of the whole was honey and he sank into a swoon.

The repeated "on her" has an authentically crude sound, but the specific descriptions are breathtaking and amusing at the same time. The parody has mocked and surpassed the tone of the original film. The story is written in brief titled sections through which the "real" and created narratives run parallel and finally mix. By an act of will, Daumier rescues Celeste from the substitute world and ends up with both her and Amelia, the moral to the story being, "The Self cannot be escaped, but it can be, with ingenuity and hard work, distracted." As in earlier stories, Barthelme offers eloquence and irony as stays against futility.

In *Great Days* (1979), the title story and many others are unnarrated dialogues, a form seen earlier in "Kierkegaard Unfair to Schlegel." In a sense, Barthelme is writing one-act plays, and the influence of Samuel Beckett, whom he admires, is not far beneath the surface. A major difference between the two, however, is that at his best Barthelme is more concerned with the nobility of his characters than with their absurdity. At their weakest, these stories are bitterly glib, such as "The Crisis." At their strongest, they become a mixture of lampoon and paean. "The Leap" subjects Kierkegaard's "leap of faith" to the kind of argument Beckett might raise; it echoes lines from *Waiting for Godot*:

—God is good and we poor are wretches who—
—Wait.

As the argument deepens, Barthelme is at his seriocomic best: "He who hath not love is a sad cookie." The nameless characters finally resolve not to act today, but soon. "Great Days" continues the focus on struggling with dignity and the importance of doing "our damnedest." The subject of this conversation-story is the agony of doing the right things while facing daily discouragement. Amid the undertow of despair and lines that bring the tension of police distress calls, come words that are both self-mocking and sincere: "I find you utterly delightful. Abide with me. We'll have little cakes with smarm, yellow smarm on them." Borrowings from a hymn title and the slang of the society set bring the speaker's aspirations down to reality and suggest that dreams for the future are not based on naivete but on sobering experience. At the conclusion, the man and woman remain, as do most of Barthelme's characters, dissatisfied. They have the only hope that Barthelme offers throughout his fiction: the solace of eloquence, the relief of irony, and the comfort of each other.

Donald Barthelme has influenced contemporary fiction, but unfortunately, he has also too often been praised for the wrong reasons. The obscurity of his work is readily visible and therefore has drawn critical praise under the label of inventiveness. His surface innovations work best when they are supported by a narrative energy and ironic humor that would strengthen any type of fiction, from the most radical to the most conservative.

• • •

The stories of Ann Beattie (1947—   ), many of which were also first published in *The New Yorker,* generally combine the realistic surface of traditional fiction and the bitter outlook typical of experimental work. Often her stories are set in New York City, or the characters are indirectly influenced by city life, but her style is not so clipped as that of other New York writers such as Grace Paley and Leonard Michaels. Her narratives flow, although in a lurching, commuter-train rhythm, and the long and short bursts finally create an underlying motion suggestive of restrained hysteria beneath a smooth surface.

Without the city, her stories tend to lose immediacy and reflective irony, which is a major problem in *Distortions* (1976). "Snake Shoes" is a good case in point. The story opens with a scene in which a character who has been telling nature myths insists, "Imagination is better than reality." Human experience is discouraging and defeating. With apparent satisfaction, Beattie's narrative voice shows none of the controlled self-mockery that often saves the work of equally bleak but more mature writers.

In *Secrets and Surprises* (1978), Beattie achieves a much more sophisticated effect in restating her themes of the need for companionship and the inevitability of alienation. "The Vintage Thunderbird" traces the on-and-off relationship of Nick and Karen through several years. They are basically symbiotic, responding to each other's weaknesses and coming back together after affairs with others. From the account of Nick's being robbed by a boy on the street prior to this story and then by two men during the story, it becomes clear that he is alone and afraid. He seeks solace in Karen's company and in her fine possessions that seem to have escaped time and danger. Thus the Thunderbird becomes enmeshed in his image of her because it is nostalgic and timeless.

When Karen says that she has sold the car, Nick becomes desperate to buy it back, as desperate as if it were his youth. The childishness of his trying to hide from the brutality of the world and the relentlessness of time is handled with humor and makes Nick likable, even pitiable. The character speaks eloquently of the urge to escape from the world into the womb of nostalgia.

"Secrets and Surprises" shows similar effective characterization and more complexity of conflict and theme. The first-person narrator is a divorcée who has moved from New York City to Connecticut. The story shows Beattie at her best in creating a sense of barely checked emotions as the narrator channels her despair between the order of language and the relief of humor. Her insecurity shows when she works through two drafts of a letter to her former husband, finally sending him a "short, funny postcard" instead. She is desolate in the country but afraid of the city. An important undercurrent of plot is the story of her retarded brother; he is a figure of human isolation, although she is even more alone. The couple who visit her also seem alone, even within their relationship. Thus life becomes a maze of secrets, with people unwilling or unable to be honest with each other, and surprises like that of her husband having left her. Her lover pleasantly surprises her when he releases a jar of lightning bugs in their bedroom, but he also tells her that he is going on tour in Europe, which will surely end their relationship. Surviving secrets and surprises is the recurrent challenge for Beattie's characters.

• • •

For the characters of Doris Betts (1932—   ), the predominant problem is lack of love. Their alienation stems from a variety of sources, but the most common solution is redemption through another human being; whereas society as a whole obliterates people, individual love helps them survive.

Whether in characters or in situations, Betts often employs the grotesque. In the settings of her stories, generally the small-town South, the imagery is vivid and economical, and her narrative often produces striking turns of phrase.

In *Beasts of the Southern Wild and Other Stories* (1973), Violet Karl, of "The Ugliest Pilgrim," transcends discouraging circumstances with a combination of faith and action that leads unexpectedly to love. As she travels from the North Carolina mountains to Oklahoma in the hope that a faith healer can remove the ax scar from her face, she meets two soldiers on the bus, and her rejection of self-pity engages them and the reader. Her determination and comic perspective make her suffering redemptive, full of unassuming nobility. In Tulsa, she mentions the many mirrors and reflecting windows where her face "is waiting in ambush" for her. When she cries with disappointment after being sent away by the healer's assistant, she explains that, because of the scar on her cheek, she "cries crooked." One of the soldiers, who claims to love her, has promised to meet her at a bus station on her way back, but since she still has the scar, she doesn't want to see him. To her surprise, he catches her when she runs from him. After their own fashion, it appears that they will live happily ever after.

The title story also presents redemption from loneliness, but without the warmth and humor that pervade "The Ugliest Pilgrim"; the world of this story is much darker and colder. "Beasts" begins with third-person narration of the story of Carol Walsh, wife, mother, and teacher, and changes to Carol's first-person viewpoint in the interwoven story of the black revolution. Apparently, the revolution provides Carol with a fantasy, including outright violence and finally concubinage. The fantasy is a relief from the dull, subjugated propriety in which she lives, and appears to be her only satisfaction. In Doris Betts's stories, characters resort to extreme behavior in their need for love.

• • •

Ray Bradbury (1920—   ) displays such skill with words and humor as to rank his stories among the best in the field of science fiction. *I Sing the Body Electric* (1969) uses standard science-fiction devices such as the time-machine truck of "The Kilimanjaro Device" and the mechanical grandmother of the title story. Both tales circumvent the limits of death: the first provides the narrator a chance to travel back in time and offer Ernest Hemingway a more fitting place in which to die, while the second supplies a substitute to children whose mother has died. The book also contains some standard "space stories."

Like its predecessors, *Long After Midnight* (1976) has its Martian stories, but the emphasis of this volume is on the characters' destructive urges. In "The Blue Bottle," a description of a decayed Martian city shows what Bradbury does best: "Sometimes towers as beautiful as a symphony would fall at a spoken word. It was like watching a Bach cantata disintegrate before your eyes." "Forever and the Earth" is a story reminiscent of "The Kilimanjaro Device"; this time Thomas Wolfe is retrieved from death. One of the best stories in the volume is "Have I Got a Chocolate Bar for You!" It is funny and true to human nature, and uses not one extreme device, making it exceptional among Bradbury's stories. A priest becomes the confessor of an obese chocolate addict, who is incidentally a Jew. Each man, in his way, helps the other in this story that is written with considerable warmth and amusement.

• • •

The stories of Herbert Gold (1929—   ) in *The Magic Will* (1971) are usually first-person narratives with little or no distinction between the storyteller's viewpoint and the author's: both usually speak their discoveries in one voice. Thus the immediacy of the works is strong.

Since there is so little difference between Gold and his characters, their lives, like his, are set in the bohemian communities of New York, San Francisco, Paris, or Haiti. He reflects on the aging of his generation and on the effects of war, career, the artist's life, divorce, love affairs, and changes in values. The recurring problem for Gold's characters is that nothing lasts—not love, family, or consolation before death. His style is simple and straightforward, and he includes a steady flow of humor in his observations.

Perhaps because of the autobiographical quality of his work, the structure is more casual than deliberate, and Gold's stories achieve their effect from mood, interesting dialogue, and detail instead of from tight, pointed structure.

Two stories that best reflect range in time and subject matter are "A Selfish Story" and "Song of the First and Last Beatnik." The former is a recollection by Herbert, the narrator, of his discovery of death; first with a classmate in a freshman literature class, while the professor spoke and they saw each other grasping what he had said; and later when the friend was killed in the war and Herbert felt his own mortality in the death of the young womanizer and fighter pilot. The nostalgia is genuine and forceful. The latter begins in San Francisco in 1957 and tells of Howard, the bohemian artist personified, a black man who began his nonconformity with the beatniks and endured through the hippies. Howard is a compulsive and flamboyant talker, but he makes sense. At the beginning he says to the narrator, "Howdya do. I got the water if you got the bucket." In his prime, he sometimes says he had the bucket *and* the water. As the story ends years later, Howard, broken by time and his society, says, "I ain't got the water." Gold ponders time and chance, which take their toll on everybody.

• • •

The characters of Shirley Ann Grau (1929—   ) in *The Wind Shifting West* (1974) are lonely and trying to adjust to unexpected change, whether they are in the yachting set of the title story or in the primitive family of "The Last Gas Station."

In the former, the sudden change in the wind and its effect on Caroline's husband, who is out sailing, parallels the change in Caroline herself, who responds to the unexpected sexual advances of her brother-in-law. The brief adventure is an act of vengeance against her husband's insistence on sailing, which she dislikes, and against his family's pressure on her to say and do the right things. Her unfaithfulness is as much an act of rebellion against her role as it is a sexual act.

The boy who is the first-person narrator of "The Last Gas Station" is a more substantial character who effectively establishes his rural innocence and his ability to handle major shocks. His oldest brother leaves home; soon afterward the father dies, then the second brother nearly kills the third in an argument and flees. When the wounded brother recovers, he too decides to leave. Finally, the narrator, who is the youngest, realizes that he will have to make his own way quite alone. He needs human contact but knows its dangers and is caught between fear and loneliness. The boy's character is well developed, and this story is representative of Grau's most powerful tales of alienation.

• • •

In his introduction to his portion of the anthology of short fiction *Fifteen by Three* (1957), James B. Hall (1918—   ) explains that, like Joyce, he is more concerned with diction and metaphor than narrative. Hall's claim for his work places the burden of proof on his use of language and imagery.

In this collection Hall's language is not especially startling, but his metaphors sometimes are, especially in the disjointed "Action Time in Twilight," where he uses five different sources of information to substitute for a narrative. In this self-consciously experimental piece, he tells his story in three first-person narratives, a doctor's reports, and letters. The result is interesting, but there is no coherent narrative to suggest what the reader should make of the decline and suicide of a madman. He refers to this story as a "studied reaction against the Laws of James," specifically, those requiring a unified narrative point of view; however, he perhaps loses as much as he gains by discarding this tradition. "In the Time of Demonstrations," a more effective story, achieves energy and insight through a church janitor's viewpoint. His understanding of a retarded man in the congregation, who, like the janitor, has suffered a life of losses, shows a brotherhood of man that is healthier outside of the church than inside.

Although the chilling alienation of his protagonists permeates Hall's stories, *Us He Devours* (1964) puts this motif to its best use. Cold, flatly written stories about a spinster bank teller ("Us He Devours"), an adolescent boy afraid of sex ("A View of the Beach"), and a compulsive gambler ("The Gambler: A Portrait of the Writer") foreshadow Raymond Carver's more barren style of the 1970s. Also like Carver, Hall occasionally relieves the bleak outlook of his work with grotesque humor, as in "The Claims Artist," in which a writer systematically dismembers himself so that he may draw workmen's compensation and be able to write full time. The price of art becomes metaphorically corporeal as the writer sees "the implication of what it was to be a writer, a really independent, nonkept, nonacademic, non-Hollywood writer." *The Short Hall* (1980) resembles the earlier collections in style. At his best, Hall writes with distinctive narration and informing irony, although he is sometimes obscure or predictable.

· · ·

For sheer volume, Joyce Carol Oates (1938—   ) has no rivals. Her stories have been published in everything from the most obscure literary quarterlies to the most sophisticated commercial magazines.

She is skillful with dialogue, perhaps her greatest strength. She sets her stories convincingly in a variety of places—the campus, city, small town, farm—and uses different organizing principles.

The world view expressed in her fiction reflects the protest and disillusionment of its era. Her characters are generally alienated and obsessed, with the result that the stories often erupt into violence and dissolve into chaos. Her fiction raises problems that it seldom probes or clarifies.

One of her most frequently mentioned stories, "Pastoral Blood" from *By the North Gate* (1963), serves as a good representative of the body of her work to date. Grace is prototypical of most of Oates's women, trapped and frustrated—

in this case, in the rigid cast of the pretty girl. Even though she is pretty, popular, and about to marry, she is alienated from her society by the role she must play. She sees impending marriage, the logical completion of this role, as the end of her life; thus she plans to commit suicide in final rebellion against the mold that restricts her. As if to kill her image before killing herself, she buys gaudy clothes, picks up a seedy-looking older man, yields to him indifferently, picks up more hitch-hikers, wrecks her new car, and finally awakens at home in bed. Realizing that she has failed to fulfill her urge for death she resolves, "All the time in the world, and next time there will be no failure. . . . Experience is the best teacher." After her decision early in the story to kill herself, nothing develops or changes significantly. There is only the superficial twist of the above quotation: rather than finding life precious after courting death, she regards it as a trap that she will escape next time. The sheer coldness of the conclusion is arresting.

Upon the Sweeping Flood (1966) continues the emphasis on alienation. In "The Survival of Childhood," Carl, an insensitive college professor, struggles to escape "blood bondage" to his rural family. He is distant in all of his relationships, including those with his wife and students. Oates skillfully sums up his attitude in the treatment of a boy in his class: "The rebuff landed on the student's face, spread itself out visibly in all directions, slumping his shoulders." He goes back to visit his family "so that he might be finally free." He also refuses the closeness his ne'er-do-well brother antagonistically calls for. During Carl's visit, the brother commits suicide, but Carl is doomed by his insensitivity to live on.

Another hopelessly self-centered character is Klein of "Archways," whose consolation is the prolonged planning of suicide. The graduate student's shame (the collective cause of which is unspecified) is so great that he enjoys making his students suffer with him, being sure that they are "educated now into knowing their unworth." His contemplation of suicide is interrupted by an affair with a student, who makes him feel "worthy of love," but love proves only a temporary, if pleasant, distraction, and he turns inward more resolutely than before, hoping for "some random incidental death."

"Upon the Sweeping Flood" takes place in Oates's often-used setting of Eden County. Walter Stuart, returning from the funeral of his father, risks his life to save two farm children from rising floodwaters. Stuart believes in the order of the world, and as a child, had "shifted his faith" from God "to the things of this world." In saving the children, he realizes that he is trying to save himself by establishing order and purpose ("they had saved him as much as he had saved them"). Then for no apparent reason, Stuart kills the boy, tries to rape the teenage girl, and acts relieved when he sights a rescue party coming in a boat. He shouts, "Save me!" as he leaves the girl, apparently wanting to be saved from himself. These protagonists are alienated, seek release, and find no comfort; they are so cold as to be unreal.

In her third collection, *The Wheel of Love and Other Stories* (1970), Oates continues along the same lines. "In the Region of Ice," an O. Henry Award winner in 1967, is one of her best stories, and the theme of alienation is apparent from the title. The central irony is that Sister Irene, who fears involvement of any sort, gets involved with Allen Weinstein. The nun and the brilliant, unstable student are outsiders who find a common ground in literature. The difference between them is that he takes literature quite seriously, wanting to reconcile thought and action, while she does not. He comes to see her after his release from a mental hospital, and says, "Give me your hand or something, touch me, help me—please." She withdraws and he soon kills himself. Her character is almost developed to fullness, though his is not, despite the potential. They are more masks for ideas than people living out the inevitable.

In "Where Are You Going? Where Have You Been?," Connie is a pretty girl who likes the power that sexual appeal gives her; the power, however, is reversed on her. In the advances of a hoodlum, complete with mirror-lens sunglasses and greasy hair, she faces the force of sex as a collective obsession. He does not have to rape her, since he can badger and lure her into submission. The irony of the situation is interesting, but the story, which is narrated mostly in dialogue, becomes repetitive, and this undercuts the tension on which it depends for its effect. Alienation persists throughout Oates's works. Repeatedly, the main character, whether man or woman, is beset by loneliness and tries to escape the agony of isolated self-awareness by means of sex, violence, or suicide. Her characters become obsessive in their attempts to escape the emptiness of their lives.

Crossing the Border (1976), *The Seduction and Other Stories* (1975), and *All the Good People I've Left Behind* (1979) continue in this vein, although the rest of Oates's collections benefit from distinct unifying concepts. In *Marriages and Infidelities* (1972), the stories are responses to classics such as Kafka's "The Metamorphosis" and Joyce's "The Dead." The stories in *The Hungry Ghosts: Seven Allusive Comedies* (1974) satirize the desperate inadequacies of academic characters. *The Goddess and Other Women* (1974) presents stories only from a feminine point of view and is largely concerned with the suppressed evil within women. Tales in *Night-Side* (1977) deal with the dark side of personality and emphasize the mystery of evil. By far the best of Oates's collections based on a theme is *The Poisoned Kiss and Other Stories from the Portuguese* (1975).

At the beginning of the book, she disclaims authorship, insisting that she received these stories from Fernandes, a Portuguese writer who, she admits, is fictitious, but whose influence she claims was vital. Obsession being her element, she uses surreal motifs to a good effect. The stories are more abstract than her usual work, and she substitutes intensity of feeling for details of surface. "The Poisoned Kiss" and "The Son of God and His Sorrow" are the best of the collection.

Joyce Carol Oates employs virtually all of the conventions for structuring fiction: internal monologue, self-conscious and unself-conscious narrators, diaries, letters, time-marked notations, "notes on contributors," even stories by a fabricated author. She also demonstrates skill in assembling her reactions to classic pieces of literature. Some critics have compared her work to Flannery O'Connor's. Although O'Connor, too, shows strange people and often writes of violence, she does so with clearly different effects. She is just as critical of the world as Oates, but the difference is that she suggests how things *should* be. O'Connor suggests what is wrong by means of narrative distance, irony, and humor. Oates does not offer a clear distinction between what her characters see and what their creator sees, leading the critical reader to recall O'Connor's warning that "Competence by itself is deadly. What is needed is the vision to go with it."

• • •

As "The Girls in their Summer Dresses" and "The Eighty-Yard Run" attest, the stories of Irwin Shaw (1913—   ) are among the finest in recent fiction; however, much of his later work is entertaining but insubstantial. *God Was Here But He Left Early* (1973) provides a good sampling in the rambling "Whispers in Bedlam" and the well-crafted "When All Things Wise and Fair Descend."

The first plays with the fanciful notion of a professional football player who changes from ordinary to brilliant because he can suddenly hear the other team's plays being called. He reaches great success, pays a heavy price, and finally asks the doctor to limit his hearing to the way it was before. The second is a conventional initiation story, complete with vivid characters, rich images and turns of phrase, and a skillfully rendered epiphany. The story first presents Steve, absolutely the all-American boy, who is well described by the comment, "No wonder he woke up feeling good." In one day, however, Steve confronts death and begins to learn compassion. The story ends aptly: "But he wasn't going to wake up, feeling automatically good, ever again."

• • •

The setting for Guy Davenport's (1927—   ) stories in *Da Vinci's Bicycle* (1979) is history itself. His works range in time from the days of Herakleitos to those of

Da Vinci, Fourier, Tatlin, and Richard Nixon. Davenport's stories seem to be primarily vehicles for ideas rather than people; they are lapidarian—cold and hard—regardless of how wisely and well they are told. By trying to make time and place universal, he often denies his reader the continuity of details that allows one to identify a place and sympathize with the characters.

One of the most accessible narratives, complete with physical details, is "John Charles Tapner." The story is also a tour de force of style; for example, the first paragraph is written with heavy alliteration and the fourth displays several invented words that call to mind James Joyce. At the remote extreme are stories like "Au Tombeau de Charles Fourier" and "A Field of Snow on a Slope of the Rosenberg." Both are disjointed and deny the reader a consistent vantage point from which to see the action.

A story from each of his two collections illustrates Davenport's style and major theme. Tatlin, in the story and volume of the same name (1974), is a Russian designer, inventor, and artist whose career begins before the Revolution and changes with it. He is Davenport's metaphor for the artist. Tatlin tries to go backward into history with his invention of the glider, to recapture childlike simplicity, both of design and spirit. Of course the state values him only for his practical skills such as designing a one-piece work suit and teaching engineering. Tatlin realizes, "It would be a disaster of the spirit were man to become mechanized in his movement."

In "The Richard Nixon Freischutz Rag" (*Da Vinci's Bicycle*), the artist is similarly misused. The story is told in parallel narratives of Nixon talking to Mao and of Da Vinci sketching his bicycle. War is the undercurrent of the story: Nixon and Mao carry on a subtly hostile conversation, while Da Vinci's bicycle is being absurdly discussed as an alternative to the horse in a cavalry charge. On a third level the narrator discusses art and history, implying that history is shaped by the bellicose and short-sighted, not the creative. With considerable skill, Davenport turns history to his purposes.

• • •

In a subtly philosophic style, Russell Banks (1940—   ) writes stories that range in setting from the West Coast to New England to the Caribbean, and in subject matter from a spoiled rich girl trying to establish her identity through sexual adventure to Simon Bolivar approaching his death. Throughout his work, memory and imagination are the consolation of his characters: memory gives them a past and a sense of order, imagination allows them to shape the formless present and future.

"Searching for Survivors (I)" the title story from his first collection (1975), begins "Poor Henry Hudson, I miss him," which states a serious theme of

Banks's work in an amusing manner. Reed, the narrator, makes broad associations between the historical figure, who surely died at sea when cast adrift by mutineers, and the dazzling Hudson car owned by his friend's father. Reed tries to preserve Hudson by believing that the explorer reached shore safely, and tries to preserve his own youth in the vision of the man with a beautifully kept car. Neither Hudson nor the father is quite what Reed makes them become by means of willful forging of memory and imagination.

The alienation of "Searching for Survivors (II)" from the same collection is much more severe. Reed, having searched the wreckage of a train and found evidence of his brother's death, cannot tell his family members, who live scattered around the country, separated by divorce and divergent adult interests. Thus the memorial service becomes a symbolic funeral for the whole family. Ironically, Reed searches for survivors but refuses to accept the dead he finds in both parts I and II of the story. "The Defenseman"—a recollection of learning to ice skate and a musing on how "the act of remembering is an act of the body"—is another story of the power of memory.

While these stories were written as acts of memory, "The New World," the title story of Banks's second collection (1978), with its self-conscious third-person narrator, explicitly addresses the importance of the creative imagination. The parallel stories of a goldsmith and a prelate in sixteenth-century Jamaica show how each man shapes his destiny and justifies his existence by the exercise of will and imagination. The prelate reiterates, "We choose our destinies," by which he excuses his constant refusal to accept a deterministic view of life even though he fails to achieve his ambitions. He, through a second-rate epic poem, and the goldsmith, through a tale he tells, justify themselves with imaginative accomplishment. The New World of the story represents the emotional wilderness in which one must live self-sustained and "must have fantasies." The Puritan mentioned by the narrator is a metaphor for the stern rationalist who rejects the consolation of imagination. Banks shows that imaginative expression enables human beings to see purpose in their efforts, redemption in their suffering.

· · ·

Much of the fiction of Paul Bowles (1911—   ) is set in Morocco (where Bowles has spent most of his writing years), some in Mexico or the Caribbean area; even those that take place in the United States have a cold, other-worldly quality. His characters always have to contend with spiritual, and usually physical, isolation. They fit into three categories: foreigners in an alien society, outcasts in their native society, or people going through a transfer of identity. His stories most often take the form of folk tales or of narratives of social conflict. The stylized texture of his writing reflects a bleak world of limitless conflict and loneliness.

Bowles first attracted attention around 1950 because of his surrealistic style, which he said resulted from "abandoning conscious control and writing whatever came from the pen." Exemplifying surrealism, "The Scorpion" tells of an old woman who lives in a cave, barely surviving. She likes her independence, but there is a man who lives in the world ouside whose attention she wants; this parallels her attitude toward society. The climactic event is her dream of swallowing a scorpion, apparently a dream of sex or death or both. "Allal" tells of an abandoned boy who trades spirits with a snake; the outcast child becomes an outcast animal, kills, and is killed.

Although Bowles has written many stark but imaginative folk tales such as these, his reputation has been largely built on stories of brutality and perversion. In "A Distant Episode," a professor studying dialects is captured by the cruelest of Bedouin tribes who rob him, cut out his tongue, and keep him as their slave and clown. He is finally sold but escapes, evidently insane. "The Delicate Prey," also set in Morocco, tells of the mutilation, rape, and killing of a boy by a member of a hostile tribe.

"Pages from Cold Point," which the narrator is self-consciously writing to the reader, created another sensation because of the implied seduction of the narrator by his son. "The Time of Friendship" is a conventional story, thus unusual in the body of Bowles's work. It is a prolonged account of the friendship of a Swiss woman and a Moroccan boy who are separated when she must leave the country and he prepares to go to war against France.

One of Bowles's best stories, "The Garden," tells of the joy a man gets from his garden, and of how his wife, then his neighbors, resent his satisfaction and turn on him. The story is an effective parable of society's intolerance of those who are self-sufficient. Even though they are simplistic, the actions have meaning.

• • •

H. E. Francis (1924—   ) has many stories that are quite traditional, some that are experimental, and others that are mixed in style. They range in setting from Long Island to Alabama to Argentina. The foreign stories tend toward sordid details and brutal action, while those in American settings have a less oppressive atmosphere, but still favor the seamy. The principal feature of his stories, whatever their style or setting, is obsession. Many protagonists are cut off from their parents by choice, circumstance, temperament, or physical distance. They are also alienated from their surroundings. Francis's characters often try to transcend their limits through seeking or suffering, both of which become obsessions. Whether they eradicate themselves by turning outward for fulfillment or inward in intense suffering, they try to escape the middle ground of normal human behavior. They look for peace in extremes, and suicide is a logical and frequent result.

The stories can be grouped according to the protagonists' obsessions. Inward-turning, which usually expresses itself as silent suffering, appears in "The Woman from Jujuy," "Trial," and "Two Lives" (the life of St. John of the Cross). Outward-turning is described in "Two Lives" (the life of an astronaut), "A Chronicle of Love," "Running," and "The Itinerary of Beggars," from the collection of that title (1973). The similarity of these apparently opposite preoccupations is pointedly shown in the parallel narratives of "Two Lives," each man being utterly absorbed in his pursuit and freed from self. Francis's command of tone distinguishes his stories, as their many voices demonstrate.

• • •

Paul Theroux (1941—   ), an expatriate American who spent considerable time in Singapore, among other places, sets most of his stories outside the United States, although his viewpoint character is usually American or British. In such places as San Juan, Bombay, and Singapore, characters confront the natives, and cultural differences are revealing. Sometimes a foreigner reacts to American culture, as in "The Love Knot." A comic story along similar lines is "Yard Sale," which concerns a Peace Corps volunteer returning to Cape Cod after two years in Samoa. He has become holier-than-thou, and criticizes all things American. Although cultural conflicts are usually severe and irreconcilable in the stories of Paul Bowles, they are generally enlightening in Theroux's work. He plays on amusing differences, and the greater the clash, the greater the humor tends to be.

Pointed satire operates in "A Political Romance," in which the main character has married a Czech woman almost as part of his doctoral program. As he loses interest in political developments in Czechoslovakia, his wife loses appeal; but when political events turn, and his specialty is back in demand, his ardor revives. The irony of an intellectual being so obtuse works well. Irony is equally strong in "Sinning with Annie." The narrator, eighty-three, an Indian, and a recent Christian convert, tells of marrying too young to be sexually capable, learning sex with his young wife, and now being resigned to celibacy for religious and physical reasons. Clearly the passion between him and his wife was a high communion and triumph. Despite having given up sex in his old age in word and deed, wholesome desire still burns in his heart.

In a very serious vein, "The Imperial Icehouse" is a parable of colonialism, a fictional analogue to Orwell's "Shooting an Elephant." A newcomer on a

Caribbean island is determined to carry ice to his plantation. He gives his workers beer in town but expects them to travel back home with him. By the end of the story, the laborers have stayed in the bar drinking for so long that the ice has melted and one of them has killed the newcomer. In "The Greenest Island," the characters are a young expatriate and the girl whom he has impregnated. Neither of them wants to marry, so finally facing a decision, they flee to San Juan, decide to return to America and put the child up for adoption, and start over separately. Like many of Theroux's characters, they have tried to escape themselves, but have matured instead.

• • •

The stories of Louis Auchincloss (1917—   ) are comfortable because they are evenly crafted, consistently realistic, and seldom surprising or disturbing. Often, as they deal with legal or social conflict, the characters tend to represent ideas or work out theories about society. The stories take place in New York City or New England.

Typical works in *Second Chance* (1970) are "Second Chance" and "The Sacrifice." The first is told through the point of view of a lawyer representing his sister-in-law in a divorce and observing the resentment of the family toward her husband. In the second, an aging judge, overwhelmed by the violence of his society, develops a nihilistic view of the world. When his grandson is murdered, the judge's despair deepens. In a twist of plot, his wife suffers a mental breakdown, leaving him independent and allowing some recovery from his despair.

Typical of Auchincloss's stories is the conflict between weak men and domineering women, a device that appears often in *The Winthrop Covenant* (1974). The Winthrop family of New England is portrayed as its members embrace and later reject the Puritan ethic. "The Covenant" is so full of exposition and religious debate that the characters are sometimes reduced to vehicles for ideas. Anne Hutchinson fulfills her "compulsion to martyrdom" and is banished. Auchincloss suggests here and elsewhere that people who live by their principles become martyrs to them, while those with weaker conviction live on in complacent hypocrisy. Either way, religion takes its toll. "The Penultimate Puritan" shows that the old order of Puritan New England is utterly gone, as demonstrated by the disintegrated family, divorce, and desertion. Although the modern descendants of the Winthrops have replaced faith in God with self-seeking ("my faith is me"), they still feel some pressure to conform and uphold the false fronts of a weakened society. The recurrent theme is that society has no place for the person of conviction.

• • •

James Alan McPherson (1943—   ) examines alienation of various sorts. The most obvious type is that of the black in white society, but he offers several variations on the problem. His black characters are misfits more because of their specific personality traits than because of their race. On this point, McPherson commendably avoids stereotype.

In *Hue and Cry* (1969), "A Matter of Vocabulary" portrays a boy learning hypocrisy first from black deacons who pocket collection money, then from whites who ignore him and will not speak to him. By the end of the story, the boy is disillusioned with both races. The problem of racial prejudice is pointedly expressed in "On Trains," in which one white woman complains about a black porter sleeping in her Pullman car, while another welcomes the black bartender into her bed. "Gold Coast" and "Of Cabbages and Kings" tell of the struggle of black intellectuals. The narrator in the first story, plagued by his own ambition and the insensitivity of the whites around him, begins to realize that he uses people as much as anyone else does.

The second story depicts the more vivid conflict of a black man trying to maintain his integrity against pressure from other blacks. Claude reverses his envy of whites and starts to speak the cant of black power, full of paranoia and hatred of established white society. Claude's friend Howard sees through the jargon but finally yields to the blind energy of Claude's views. Intellect succumbs to passion. The complexity of Howard's confusion and acquiescence is convincingly drawn. "The Faithful," from *Elbow Room* (1977), also shows a black man caught in social changes he cannot cope with. John Butler, preacher and barber, suffers the shock of having both his preaching and his barbering rejected and he refuses to adapt.

• • •

Because he shares their New York setting and their sense of comic absurdity, Leonard Michaels (1933—   ) can be compared to Grace Paley and Donald Barthelme. Beyond these surface similarities, however, the differences are great. Michaels' stories are usually built around characters and situations that begin in the realm of the believable and proceed to the outrageous, sometimes the surreal. Although not all of his stories are comic, his most distinctive and memorable ones are. The context is often New York, usually the city's Jews whose problems often stem from sexual desire. The style is marked by abrupt, short sentences that hang together with a vitality and logical progression that save his style from being choppy. In fact, they are not unlike the routine of a stand-up comedian, full of related one-liners.

"City Boy," from *Going Places* (1969), illustrates the point. This is one of the most profoundly funny stories in recent years, mainly because every bit of absurdity has believable origins. Beginning with the obvious comic potential of a father discovering his daughter and her boyfriend entangled on the floor at 3:00 a.m., Michaels never relents. First the father stumbles in the dark and steps on the boy's bare buttocks. The boy runs from the apartment nude, panicked, but somewhat encouraged by the thought that this was a real breakthrough with the father, who spoke to him for the first time during the misadventure. He decides to walk down the street on his hands, as if the only response to the situation is absurd bravado. What the boy says and thinks is ridiculous, but no more so than so-called reasonable behavior would be in his desperate circumstances. Several other stories in this volume treat the problems of sex and guilt; some are in the nearly traditional style of "City Boy" ("Crossbones" and "Sticks and Stones"), and others, less effectively, are attempts at surrealism ("Making Changes" and "Mildred").

I Would Have Saved Them If I Could (1975) follows the linear plot form of *Going Places* and the stories present far more believable actions ("Murderers," "Mackerel," and "Reflections of a Wild Kid," for example). The departure from the norm in this collection is not in incident, but in structure. "Eating Out" is a series of very short sketches that deal ironically with ambition, sexual needs, and failure of communication. Similarly, "I Would Have Saved Them If I Could" is a set of sketches that shows examples of suffering and loss. It has the effect of ritual acceptance of death and grief, but the self-mocking tone prevents the story from concluding in a whine. Irony, as used in "Reflections of a Wild Kid," allows characters to focus on the grim without yielding to despair. Michaels uses pity and humor to offer insight.

•   •   •

Even though his style is simple and his presentation is realistic, Hugh Nissenson (1933—   ) does not become ordinary or dull, because his characters confront interesting moral conflicts, both internal and vis-a-vis each other. Most of the stories of *In the Reign of Peace* (1972) are set in Israel from 1946 to 1970, and good illustrations of his work are "The Throne of Good" and the title story.

In the first, a doctor must choose between protecting a young Zionist who is on an assassination mission, and turning him over to the authorities before he dies of pneumonia. Although he sympathizes with the cause, he objects to both the mission and the official disregard for the boy's life. When the doctor finally decides to turn him in, the boy has fled. The doctor, who is also the narrator, asks, "Can any good come of it?" Free or captured, the boy will inevitably kill or be killed. Death begets death, endlessly.

The turmoil of the second story is religious rather than political. Chaim, a Moroccan laborer, has a strong religious faith, while few members of the Israeli kibbutz on which he works believe in anything and cannot understand why Chaim does. Chaim calls the narrator to see a trapped mouse being eaten alive by ants; to him, this illustrates the agonies that he expects will be alleviated by the coming of the Messiah. Chaim, with his simple but genuine faith that there is ultimate order and justice, serves as a rebuke to the rest who appear to have a purpose but feel no consolation. The contest of divided loyalties and a mixture of hope and despair enrich this collection.

· · ·

Only eight of *The Complete Stories* (1971) of Flannery O'Connor (1925—1964) did not appear earlier in her two collections or, in an altered form, within her two novels. Of these eight, "The Partridge Festival" was written and published much later, and "Why Do the Heathen Rage?" was the beginning of a novel, even though it was published as a story. O'Connor clearly did not intend to have the latter appear except as part of the novel; she withdrew the former after submitting it as part of *Everything That Rises Must Converge* (1965), and she made no effort to get the others published in a volume. Therefore one cannot expect her usual compression and brilliance in these works. Still, the character of Old Dudley of "The Geranium" shows signs of what O'Connor was to achieve later, and "The Partridge Festival" contains pleasing, if heavy-handed, irony. Even O'Connor's weaker stories have substance.

· · ·

Look How the Fish Live (1975), is a collection of stories about family life and Catholic priests, the traditional subjects of J. F. Powers (1917—   ). Control of narrative distance and incisive use of humor are the consistent strengths of his work. The theme of his stories is conflict, usually over everyday matters, that represent the characters' attitudes toward deeper things. Stories dealing with priests are intensified rather than trivialized by the restrictions of clerical life.

Two stories illustrate how irony is sharpened when it is applied to ethical context. "Bill" details the frustration of a mediocre pastor who drinks too much, spends his time thinking about new furniture, and looks forward to obtaining a curacy. The curate himself is cold and independent, and only exacerbates the pastor's loneliness and sense of failure. "One of Them" reverses the situation; this story is told from the viewpoint of the curate, a convert, who strains to be accepted by his aloof pastor. Although concerned with the church, "Pharisees" is an unusual story for Powers because it is nonrealistic in its use of characters and dialogue. The characters who confront each other in a diner are types who are given the roles of Pharisee, ex-Pharisee, and so on. The ex-Pharisee, a resigned priest-turned-secular humanist, pontificates more ineffectually than the Pharisees of Christ's day. Thus the most dangerous hypocrites are those who claim to have escaped hypocrisy by rejecting the church, but still don't minister to the needs of people.

In general, stories of family life are weaker than the church stories, but "Look How the Fish Live" is a notable exception. In dealing with a fallen baby dove that his children bring him, the father complains of the lack of order in nature, but finally faces his deeper complaint—that death is part of the order of nature. The design that he calls faulty is complete and relentless.

Powers is skillful in raising significant moral questions from small problems and handling his material with such control that it remains fresh and interesting.

• • •

Modesty is a distinguishing feature in the stories of Isaac Bashevis Singer (1909—   ). His stories, written in Yiddish and then translated, seem to treat simple subjects, but they are, in fact, profound. With his unassuming style, he sharpens the edges of the moral conflicts faced by characters trying to be true to themselves and loyal to their community.

Singer frequently writes about struggling writers and about young people wrestling with religious faith and ethnic loyalty. In *A Friend of Kafka and Other Stories* (1970), the title story and "Schloimele" depict the problems of unsuccessful men in Warsaw and New York, respectively. In the first, Jacques Kohn says that he is suffering the same crippling hypersensitivity that his friend Kafka did: "No defect can be hidden from me. That is impotence." Kohn sees fate as his opponent in a long, slow game to the death, but by telling a friend of his past, he preserves his identity. The narrator of the second story, apparently Kohn's friend, now older and in America, hopes to have one of his stories produced as a play by the grand-talking Schloimele. Schloimele, however, only makes promises and disappears, and the narrator realizes, "Schloimele symbolized for me wasted time, my own failure." After many years they do get together, and the narrator sees how old and broken Schloimele has become—until he smiles and talks of his latest hopes. In both of these stories, men save themselves from despair by sheer determination.

"The Crown of Feathers" and "Grandfather and Grandson" illustrate the second type of story in *The Crown of Feathers and Other Stories* (1973). In the first, the favored granddaughter of a wealthy man renounces Judaism and returns to it, but suffers greatly because of her uncertainty. She needs her search, however, even more than the answers she longs for. The story concludes, "Because if there is such a thing as truth, it is as intricate and hidden as a crown of feathers." The second story, set in Warsaw, shows the conflict between a grandfather's spiritual view of the world (Judaism) and his grandson's atheistic approach (Bolshevism). Each is sincere and argues cogently, and neither yields. The boy is killed by the Russians, thus demonstrating that his cause has only temporary remedies for permanent problems. Faith in the eternal and in ultimate justice sustains the grandfather in his grief. The weight of the past and the necessity of choice pervade Singer's stories.

• • •

Cynthia Ozick (1928—   ), in *The Pagan Rabbi and Other Stories,* (1971) and *Bloodshed and Three Novellas,* (1976), writes with particular strength about Jews facing religious and social conflicts. In this regard her stories resemble those of Singer. Ozick's style is not so deliberately simple, but her concern with Jews who cannot wholly accept the faith (the "pagan rabbi" who hangs himself) or wholly reject it (the skeptic in "Bloodshed" who visits a remote Hasidic community) reminds the reader of Singer. In "Envy," part of her first collection, she even has a Singer-like character, who writes in Yiddish and has had great success with translations of his work. The viewpoint character, full of valid objections to and blind envy of the successful writer, is an artful mixture of frustrated failure and truth-teller. The story comments on the fragility of worthy literature and the mindless fads that exalt the ordinary and subdue the excellent. All of Ozick's stories have a ponderous tone—a virtually unrelieved seriousness—as she presents grim and convincing accounts of people suffering the trials of faith, doubt, and art.

• • •

The three volumes of Frederick Busch (1941—   ) display progressive development in compression of narrative, effectiveness of characterization, and resonance of theme. An acute fear of death pervades the stories. Anxiety comes from facing death itself or from facing the next thing to it—hopeless isolation. The family, both an emotional and biological means of combatting death, figures prominently, with characters' hopes directly related to their families, or how to manage without one.

The title story of *Breathing Trouble* (1973), although uneven, is the best of the volume. A man who is obese, divorced, and anxiety-ridden has "breathing trouble," the story's metaphor. His illness, plus that of an orphaned asthmatic boy, represents (and largely stems from) his fear of loneliness and death. The boy is more a symbol than a character, and the narrative is needlessly obscure. Other stories in the collection depict more characters isolated by divorce and death.

Domestic Particulars (1976) follows the life of one family from 1919 to 1976, with Claire Miller and her son Harry as focal characters. The author's clear purpose is to show the pain of alienation within the family. In "The Goal of Life Is Death," Harry Miller recovers from a heart attack and subsequently muses on the meaning of his life. He speaks of himself as the "child who fled because families are—write it down, it's a definition—what you finally have to leave." He has left his parents so that he can start a family of his own. Harry recalls holding his own infant son and laments the passing of his child's youth just as his parents lamented the passing of his. He encounters the cycle of life and death from its very center, the family.

In dealing with a community instead of one family, *Hardwater Country* (1979) also regards death, but on a broader scale. The stories tell of families or of characters without families. In "Widow Water," a plumber, the man who can handle the mysterious life force of water, shows how people face helplessness, whether it is the result of well problems or deeper fears. The death image in "What You Might As Well Call Love" is not in the failure of wells, but in ceaseless rain. The specific threat of a flooded basement represents those forces people cannot control, such as death itself. Through the use of mundane images, this collection presents a vivid panorama of people resisting death.

• • •

In recent years, writers rejecting the middle way of traditional fiction have chosen obscurity, taking the risk of baffling the reader in the hope that they can surprise and delight. Raymond Carver (1938—   ), however, has elected instead to use utter simplicity. Typical are "They're Not Your Husband," "The Fling," and "Will You Please Be Quiet, Please?," the title story from his first collection (1976). Like most of Carver's fiction, they tell of a contest with loneliness. In "Will You Please Be Quiet, Please?," the husband, finally getting up his nerve, asks his wife if she had committed adultery two years before. She confesses; he hits her and leaves. When he returns home the next morning, she tries to talk, but he refuses to listen. She offers her body instead of words, and in spite of himself, he responds. The story seems to say that the physical man can overpower, and sometimes reconcile, the rational man, but it has too little detail and the dialogue is unrevealing.

Carver can round out his stories, as seen in "Bicycles, Muscles, Cigarettes" and "Distance." The first is sketchy but still vivid in such details as the smell of nicotine, which carries the hint of mortality for the protagonist. The narrative persona of "Distance" gives perspective on events, as a father tells his grown daughter about a day before he and her mother were divorced. In the particulars of the young couple's argument and reconciliation, the sweetness of that time is revived: "They danced, and then they held to each other as if there would always be that morning."

• • •

Daniel Curley (1918—   ) is a good example of the writer who is both traditional and experimental. Stories in Curley's first two volumes are traditional, while in the third book there is a mixture. The benchmark of his work is a sense of loss, whether it is disillusionment, aging, or death. Although some of his stories are thoroughly bleak, most have a steady current of humor that makes grave losses bearable and trivial ones interesting.

"Saccovanzetti," from *That Marriage Bed of Procrustes* (1957), uses a boys' game as a means to contemplate death. Mickey is repeatedly made to play the victim. Feeling the injustice of this, he knows that if he is ever to be one of the game's survivors, he will have to "outwit and outshoot those who could not be outwitted and outshot." Sacco and Vanzetti will be executed that night, and Mickey, the story's metaphor for mortal man, must accept the role he has been assigned. (He does avenge himself on his brother by talking of throwing the switch on the electric chair, then flushing the toilet on which his brother sits).

Characters face death in more serious terms in "The Night of the Two Wakes." Students working in a restaurant go first to a wake for the dishwasher's mother and then to one for a fellow worker who drowned. At both they try to show appropriate respect; still there is a limit to how well they can either fathom death or sustain adult behavior. "That Marriage Bed of Procrustes" tells of the pain of maturity besetting George and Alice Fuller. They agree that their life together is "no use," and George says, referring to the loss of innocence, "I have never since entered a mystery that didn't disappoint me."

The losses faced in middle age are the focus of "Where You Wouldn't Want to Walk" from *In the Hands of Our Enemies* (1970). While walking in the woods with a young woman, the narrator falls and suffers a slipped disc, which is symbolic of physical as well as imaginative limits. The story ends with the narrator frustrated and isolated. In terms explicitly reminiscent of Dostoyevsky, "A Story of Love, Etc." shows life as an inevitable compromise. A mixture of first-person and third-person narration describes a woman who prostitutes herself, with the knowledge of her husband, as a means of surviving the Depression. The narrator links compromise and redemption when he compares the woman to Sonia Marmeladov of *Crime and Punishment,* who "is also Jesus Christ crucified and saving the world."

Most of the stories in *Love in the Winter* (1976) are experimental, the later ones especially difficult to understand because of disjointed narrative. "What Rough Beast?" is an exception, since the vague description of the beast heightens the suspense and underlines the main character's need to be able to see and identify mortal danger.

"Who, What, When, Where—Why?" is pure metafiction. It is a writer telling a story about telling a story, and it exhibits a vividness and narrative drive that most metafiction lacks. The narrator is irresistibly candid and funny, and he establishes an effective fictional world despite his claim that it is real. Even though this account of a drunken night in Birmingham, Alabama, has an inconclusive ending, the story is effective as a device for seeking the truth of experience. The title story, also written with vivid and amusing turns of phrase, tells of a middle-aged college professor who finds himself unable to commit adultery as he set out to do. The story ends with him grieving over his lost nerve and lost youth. Curley writes with humor and variety on the subject of loss.

• • •

The stories of Andre Dubus (1936—   ), both in *Separate Flights* (1975) and in *Adultery and Other Choices* (1977), tend to deal with marital conflicts or youthful initiation experiences. Although Dubus has written good stories on other subjects, his most characteristic stories are in these two areas. The title story of each collection is a detailed treatment of an atrophied marriage from the viewpoint of the frustrated wife; in the first, she yields to futility, while in the second, she grows beyond her self-centered husband and decides to divorce him. In both, Dubus deftly portrays mixed feelings and divided loyalties.

The initiation stories dwell on the fears, guilt, and ambition of Paul Clement, a Catholic boy who goes to parochial school in Louisiana. He suffers with sexual desires and a test of his faith ("If They Knew Yvonne"); faces conflict with his father and gains a deepened understanding of him to the point that he defends his father's right to upbraid his foolishness ("Contrition"); and endures Marine Corps boot camp to win his own respect as well as his father's ("Cadence").

• • •

Many of the stories of Philip F. O'Connor (1932—   ) deal with insanity or pathologic despair, such as "Donovan, the Cat Man" and "Mastodon's Box" in *Old Morals, Small Continents, Darker Times* (1971), and "The Escape Artist" and "The Pony Track" in *A Season for Unnatural Causes* (1975)). The alienated characters in these stories tend to identify themselves in terms of the society as a whole. The reader sees much of what is wrong with these people but sees little of the people themselves: the author describes the disorders, not their victims.

O'Connor's best work is in a familial or ethnic context. His stories of family conflict have the vividness of intimate struggle; those of extreme alienation have flat language, drab settings, and predictably bleak endings. Both achieve memorable characterization. From the first collection, "The Gift Bearer" and "My Imaginary Father" are about the fights in an Irish family between a drinking father and a harsh mother, as seen by their son. "Story Hour" is told from the viewpoint of a similarly vulnerable boy who indirectly witnesses the suicide of a priest who had been a chaplain in the war and supposedly a wounded hero. The wound was psychological, and the faith the priest has exemplified is not strong enough to save him. The tension in such stories gives substance to character and theme.

The stories in the second collection tell predominantly of utter alienation. A notable and strong exception is "The Disciple," in which a Catholic boy struggles with the temptations of the flesh within a well-drawn religious framework. Others, such as "Other Lives" and "The Thumb," focus on alienation more than on an alienated human being. The stories are experimental in their use of disjointed narrative.

• • •

Grace Paley (1922—   ) had a reputation for manipulating language and structure for effect well before 1960. Thus the experimental surface of the stories in *Enormous Changes at the Last Minute* (1974) was nothing new to her readers. The style is terse, establishing a rhythm suitable to the New York City setting of her stories. The language combines humor and tension, especially in "Wants," "Debts," and "Enormous Changes at the Last Minute," in which principal characters are alienated from their families.

Paley relies on word play and tone to create atmosphere, and largely ignores physical details. In "Wants," the first-person narrator feels dislocated and lost in time as she realizes that her hopes have not matured along with the trees of the city. She complains, ". . . I don't understand how time passes," and does not know where her life has gone. Paley places more faith in the power of tropes than in realistic details. The narrator describes her former husband, not by physical features, but by an image: "He had had a habit throughout the twenty-seven years of making a narrow remark which, like a plumber's snake, could work its way through the ear down the throat halfway to my heart."

Repeatedly, time brings losses, and only language gives time's victims a means to clarify and preserve experience. The narrator of "Debts," a writer, says of her subjects that she wants "to tell their stories . . . to save a few lives." By telling a story within her story and distorting reality to her purposes, she implies that every story is worth telling, regardless of how many facts may have to be made up. The result is a theoretical comment about fiction rather than vivid characterization.

Alexandra, of "Enormous Changes at the Last Minute," is caught between the past and present. The opposing poles are represented by her father (old sense: speaking from his hospital bed, telling her that she is killing him) and by Dennis (new frenzy: hippie, rock musician, free-lover). She sees the folly of Dennis and his notion that his generation is revolutionary beyond all others, but she also understands the worth of his energy, humor, and vitality. The story runs the risk of being a trite tale of the liberated woman, and the song motif, which is contrived, emphasizes its weakness.

• • •

In his fiction, Richard Stern (1928—   ) uses humor to strip human experience to the bare bones of despair, then fleshes out the figure again. His insight arrests, enlightens, and grudgingly consoles. His narrators and characters often say what many people have felt but could not say, because the perception to grasp difficult problems and the courage to describe them seldom come at the same time. The combination of keen sight and candid telling creates epiphanies that burst forth in short declarative sentences.

One story from each collection will illustrate Stern's technique. As the title suggests, *1968* (1970) examines American society by telling the stories of various people during the turbulent year. In many ways, Holleb of "Ins and Outs" is Stern's representative man, whose accomplishment never matches his vision. This vision is a handicap because it reduces him to Prufrock's despair, seeing but not acting. The story begins with an exceptionally funny scene devoted to Holleb's respiratory problems, which symbolize his overwhelming petty concerns. He summarizes his life: "Marriage: over. Son: miserable. Apartment: in bad shape. Work: third-rate. Books: unwritten. Victimizer: uncaught." His despair deepens when a black man beats him solely because he is white. He finally sympathizes with the frustration of his attacker, but decides to press charges in court if the man is caught, because seeing things through is necessary in a life that is already compromising. Thus, having experienced both personal and impersonal grief and still survived, he presses on.

Turning from society in general to the family in particular, the title story from *Packages* (1980) treats death with determined irreverence. In this story, as well as the others in the collection, Stern's characters are cut off from each other. The narrator of "Packages" spares no one: the undertaker—"Campbell's is a wonderful funeral factory"; his deceased mother—"My mother was not my type." A mixture of grief and bitterness churns through the story, implying that if the narrator did admit how much he loved his mother, he could not face the sorrow. He carries around a package containing his mother's ashes and tries to escape her by throwing it into a garbage truck. But he cannot shed his grief, and his inability to numb himself is the hope with which the story ends. Stern razes and rebuilds, starting stories in confusion, ending them in clarity.

• • •

Like most recent serious writers, Barry Targan (1932—   ) has written at length of death and alienation; but unlike most, he offers redemption. In a world that presumably knows better than to hope for heroes, Targan writes stories with subtle, vivid heroes. His people fight—each other sometimes, but more often their own fears and limitations. Sometimes they only win their self-respect. More often, however, they jar and invigorate others with their battles.

Not all of Targan's stories have heroes, and some that do sink into sentimentality. In *Harry Belton and the Mendelssohn Violin Concerto* (1975), the stories without heroes tend to be flat and forgettable, like "Leaving" and "Leave My Mother Alone." In "The Clay Wars" and "And Their Fathers Who Begat Them," the concluding heroism is pure and pronounced, rather like that found in children's tales. These lapses, however, do not negate the force that is usually under control in his work: determination to sketch scenes of discovery for people who matter to the reader.

The art of Targan's stories is his controlled treatment of sentimental material, a risk few contemporary writers are willing to take. The main character of "Harry Belton and the Mendelssohn Violin Concerto" is a mediocre amateur violinist determined to perform in a concert hall. Considering the expense, hard work, and probable embarrassment, everyone discourages him; but he performs, makes mistakes, recovers admirably, and even plays an encore. Even though it is a clear, conventional narrative like the rest of Targan's stories, "Elizabeth Lanier" develops one of the strangest and most intriguing plots in recent fiction. The narrator finds himself about to be seduced by the beautiful Elizabeth Lanier, then beaten by her brother as his friends have been. Surely there is no more clearly defined approach-avoidance situation in any psychology book. He accepts Elizabeth's offer, then faces her brother and beats him. Simple enough, but the boy tells truths that are seldom spoken these days: "Dread is the worst of punishments," and at the end of the story, "Only this I know, there *is* victory and defeat. . . . For to have once won enormously and well is searing, a hot kindling of light, an illumination ever after as though you have no choice any more to ever lose or lie dark again."

Targan also creates heroes who do not win, but they still have their reward. "In Excelsis Deo" and "Kingdoms," from *Surviving Adverse Seasons* (1979), both have main characters who discover the cruelty of death and become obsessed with it. The stories present a bleak view of the human condition, but Targan never yields to the glib cynicism that often marks Beattie and Barthelme. Instead, the two men who are eager for answers, no matter what the price, learn to live with disillusionment and acceptance of pain. A widowed father tells his son, "The gods are not just. But they are *right*."

• • •

Like all of the stories of Peter Taylor (1917—   ) those in *In the Miro District and Other Stories* (1977) are rich in nuance. He depicts his world in a clear narrative voice and with revealing details, so that every statement and gesture carries more than surface meaning.

Four of these stories are in verse, particularly appropriate in "The Instruction of a Mistress," which consists of journal entries by a poet and a letter by the woman he discarded. The stories are most often set in Nashville, some quite vividly in the period from 1900 to the Depression; their milieu is one in which decorum is not a petty matter but a worthy concern of self-disciplined people. The importance of familial relations and social responsibility is especially pronounced.

In "The Captain's Son," the title character tries to expiate the failure of his father, only to fall prey, as if by biblical prophecy, to the same weaknesses. "The Hand of Emmagene," another verse story, tells of a country girl in the city who misinterprets the demands of her hostess and destroys herself. On the simplest level, "In the Miro District" is the story of a generation gap; deeper, it shows how a rift between a grandson and grandfather makes the old Civil War veteran see his own emptiness, despair of maintaining integrity, and yield to the superficial role his society wants him to play. With elegant language, Taylor's stories dwell on the difficulty of balancing inner needs and outer duties.

· · ·

With the exceptions of *Bech: A Book* (1970), and *Museums and Women and Other Stories* (1972), the post-1969 collections of John Updike (1932—   ) focus primarily on married life and the related affairs, separations, and divorces that often attend marriage in modern America. In isolation, older stories such as "Pigeon Feathers," "A. & P.," and "In Football Season" are impressive, but as a body of work, his Maples stories and the many others dealing with varying stages of romantic harmony and discord are especially fine. Updike details the agony, humor, and regret of people trying to disengage unreasoning links of love and resentment, showing emotional turmoil so vividly that the worth of his characters magnifies as their confusion grows. With exact description and dialogue, he subjects his characters to pain and then makes it tolerable with humor and eloquence.

The main character of *Bech: A Book* is Henry Bech, a novelist who succeeded with his first novel, wrote quite poorly thereafter, and finally is faced with growing fame (belated, and now undeserved) and a writer's block. *Bech* and *Too Far to Go* (1979) have been called novels, and with some cause, but the stories in both stand alone well. The former, which has been widely and justly applauded, looks more at the relationship of the artist to society than at broader human experience.

Aside from the essays and experimental pieces in *Museums and Women,* most of the stories anticipate the style Updike uses in later collections. Early in "Museums and Women" the first-person narrator says of the mother—and, by extension, of all women—"Who she was was a mystery so deep it never formed into a question." And so the story continues: for all that they can be perceived and sensed, museums and women raise more questions than they answer. "When Everyone Was Pregnant" centers on the ripeness of young parenthood and on the excesses of guiltless youth in the 1950s. The first-person narrator explains that people then "Viewed the world through two lenses since discarded: fear and gratitude." Both bespeak a humility lost in the America of the 1970s. Trying to decide why that era, when all of their friends and he and his wife were having their children, is so precious in his memory, the narrator reflects on Shakespeare's "Ripeness is all" and decides that it means, "Ripeness is God." Finally he faces the lessons of youth, mutability, and death that have passed before him: "The decades slide seaward, taking us along. I am still afraid. Still grateful."

As the above passages suggest, John Updike is a master of the elegant phrase in contemporary American short fiction. He is also considerably more: a master of the substance of short stories who can employ imagery, humor, and dialogue to rivet and delight his reader. Perhaps the most vivid illustration of this appears in "Domestic Life in America" from *Problems and Other Stories* (1979). Symbolizing his failed efforts to sustain his recently dissolved marriage, the main character visits the house that used to be his and replaces "several of the stones of the little retaining wall he had built here in hopes of giving an amorphous area order." His marriage was his retaining wall. Humor mixes with grief as he recalls how his dog wagged her tail while he measured her for a grave before putting her to sleep. Self-mockery holds back sentimentalism as he recalls the dog's burial: "It appeared to him through his absurd, excessive tears that he was burying a dozen golden summers, his children's childhood and his own blameless prime." Updike's dialogue sharpens the rough edges smoothed by humor when his daughter accuses, "If you want to be so useful why don't you live with us?" Updike's dialogue sometimes overwhelms the reader with abruptly stated truths. "Problems" deals further with the complications of divorce, but in the format of mathematical word problems: "During the night, A, though sleeping with B, dreams of C," and later, "A's psychiatrist thinks he is experiencing growth. . . . However, by Tristan's Law appealingness is inversely proportional to attainability." The tone achieved is a blend of humor and frustration. With inventive wit, Updike states qualitative problems in quantitative terms to show that reason is useless in matters of the heart.

As a whole piece, *Too Far to Go* (1979) is Updike's finest collection, and if one values thought and feeling in literature, it must be one of the best since World War II.

"Wife-wooing" displays bursts of poetic language, such as, "Seven years since I wed wide warm woman, white-thighed. Wooed and wed. Wife. A knife of a word that for all its final bite did not end the wooing. To my wonderment." Of course, the alliteration here is heavy, even a parody; but beneath the arch surface, the words are expressive. Trying to talk himself out of his enduring love for his wife, the narrator later watches morning light as it "drains the goodness from your thickness. . . . I feast with the coffee on your drabness," a blunt counterpoint to the earlier passage. To his surprise and joy, a day of fault-finding is undone that night "with a kiss of toothpaste to me moist and girlish and quick; the momentous moral of this story being, An unexpected gift is not worth giving." Intervening stories describe passionate married love and infidelities, as Richard and Joan Maples pull reluctantly apart and uncertainly back together. "Gesturing" follows the separation of the couple, and the focal image of the story is a movement of Joan's as she "tentatively, soundlessly, tapped the fingers of one hand into the palm of the other, a gesture between a child's clap of glee and an adult's signal for attention, 'I've decided to kick you out.'" The end of the story reveals what living separately and having other lovers has taught them: "that these lovers, however we love them, are not us, are not sacred as reality is sacred. We are reality. We have made children. We gave each other our young bodies. We promised to grow old together." In the stories of John Updike great eloquence kindles simple warmth.

•   •   •

As America in the 1960s and 1970s changed faster and with less unity of purpose than in the previous decades, so did the short story. The experimental theorists, questioning the adequacy of old forms to describe a radically new world, jarred traditional writers into a more self-conscious pursuit of their art. Conversely, the traditional writers questioned the worth of what experimentalists had produced when their declarations of theory were finished. The conflict stimulated the members of both camps; and finally, most writers, finding their own way and working out their own ideas and styles, took whatever suited them from both approaches. By 1980, the tug of war in short fiction had reached somewhat of an equipoise in which neither radicalism nor conservatism was the crucial feature of a story. Regardless of how a writer achieved it, resonance of thought and feeling was still paramount.

James C. Robison

Belmont College

Selected Bibliography of American Short Story Collections: 1945—1980

Abel, Robert. *Skin and Bones.* Fort Collins: Colorado State University Press, 1979.

Abish, Walter. *Minds Meet.* New York: New Directions, 1975.

Adams, Alice. *Beautiful Girl.* New York: Knopf, 1978.

Adler, Warren. *The Sunset Gang.* New York: Viking, 1977.

Algren, Nelson. *The Last Carousel.* New York: Putnam, 1973.

———. *Neon Wilderness.* Garden City, N.Y.: Doubleday, 1947.

Allen, Woody. *Side Effects.* New York: Random House, 1980.

Apple, Max. *The Oranging of America and Other Stories.* New York: Viking, 1976.

Auchincloss, Louis, *The Injustice Collectors.* Boston: Houghton Mifflin, 1950.

———. *The Partners.* Boston: Houghton Mifflin, 1974.

———. *Powers of Attorney.* Boston: Houghton Mifflin, 1963.

———. *The Romantic Egoists: A Reflection in Eight Minutes.* Boston: Houghton Mifflin, 1954.

———. *Second Chance: Tales of Two Generations.* Boston: Houghton Mifflin, 1970.

———. *Tales of Manhattan.* Boston: Houghton Mifflin, 1967.

———. *The Winthrop Covenant.* Boston: Houghton Mifflin, 1976.

Baker, Carlos. *The Talismans and Other Stories.* New York: Scribner's, 1976.

Baldwin, James. *Going to Meet the Man.* New York: Dial, 1965.

Ballard, James. *Rolling All the Time.* Urbana: University of Illinois Press, 1976.

Bambara, Toni Cade. *The Sea Birds Are Still Alive: Collected Stories.* New York: Random House, 1977.

Banks, Russell. *The New World.* Urbana: University of Illinois Press, 1978.

———. *Searching for Survivors.* Brooklyn, N.Y.: Fiction Collective, 1975.

Barth, John. *Lost In the Funhouse: Fiction for Print, Tape, Live Voice.* Garden City, N.Y.: Doubleday, 1968.

Barthelme, Donald. *Amateurs.* New York: Farrar, Straus & Giroux, 1976.

———. *City Life.* New York: Farrar, Straus & Giroux, 1970.

———. *Come Back, Dr. Caligari.* Boston: Little, Brown, 1964.

———. *Great Days.* New York: Farrar, Straus & Giroux, 1979.

———. *Guilty Pleasures.* New York: Farrar, Straus & Giroux, 1974.

————. *Sadness*. New York: Farrar, Straus & Giroux, 1972.

————. *Unspeakable Practices, Unnatural Acts*. New York: Farrar, Straus & Giroux, 1968.

Baumbach, Jonathan. *The Return of Service*. Urbana: University of Illinois Press, 1979.

Beck, Warren. *The Blue Sash, and Other Stories*. Yellow Springs, Ohio: Antioch Press, 1941.

————. *The Far Whistle, and Other Stories*. Yellow Springs, Ohio: Antioch Press, 1951.

————. *The First Fish, and Other Stories*. Yellow Springs, Ohio: Antioch Press, 1951.

————. *The Rest Is Silence, and Other Stories*. Denver: Swallow, 1963.

Bellow, Saul. *Mosby's Memoirs, and Other Stories*. New York: Viking, 1968.

————. *Seize The Day: With Three Short Stories and A One-Act Play*. New York: Viking, 1956.

Betts, Doris. *The Astronomer and Other Stories*. New York: Harper, 1965.

————. *Beasts of the Southern Wild and Other Stories*. New York: Harper, 1973.

————. *The Gentle Insurrection and Other Stories*. New York: Putnam, 1954.

Bingham, Sallie. *The Touching Hand and Six Short Stories*. Boston: Houghton Mifflin, 1967.

————. *The Way it Is Now: Stories*. New York: Viking, 1972.

Bovey, John. *Desirable Aliens*. Urbana: University of Illinois Press, 1980.

Bowles, Jane. *The Collected Works of Jane Bowles*. New York: Farrar, Straus & Giroux, 1966.

————. *My Sister's Hand in Mine*. New York: Ecco, 1978.

Bowles, Paul. *Collected Stories 1939—1976*. Santa Barbara: Black Sparrow, 1980.

————. *The Delicate Prey and Other Stories*. New York: Random House, 1950.

————. *A Hundred Camels in the Courtyard*. San Francisco: City Lights, 1962.

————. *Let it Come Down*. New York: Random House, 1952.

————. *Things Gone and Things Still Here*. Santa Barbara: Black Sparrow, 1977.

————. *Three Tales*. New York: F. Hallman, 1975.

————. *The Time of Friendship: A Volume of Short Stories*. New York: Holt, 1967.

Boyle, Kay. *The Crazy Hunter: Three Short Novels*. New York: Harcourt, 1940.

————. *Fifty Stories*. New York: Doubleday, 1980.

————. *The Smoking Mountain: Stories of Postwar Germany*. New York: McGraw-Hill, 1951.

————. *Thirty Stories*. New York: Simon & Schuster, 1946.

Boyle, T. Coraghessan. *Descent of Man*. Boston: Little, Brown, 1979.

Bradbury, Ray. *Dark Carnival*. Sauk City, Wis.: Arkham House, 1947.

————. *Fahrenheit 451*. New York: Simon & Schuster, 1967.

————. *The Golden Apples of the Sun*. Garden City, N.Y.: Doubleday, 1953.

————. *I Sing the Body Electric! Stories*. New York: Knopf, 1969.

————. *The Illustrated Man*. Garden City, N.Y.: Doubleday, 1951.

————. *Long after Midnight*. New York: Knopf, 1976.

————. *The Machineries of Joy: Short Stories*. New York: Simon & Schuster, 1964.

————. *The Martian Chronicles*. Garden City, N.Y.: Doubleday, 1958.

————. *A Medicine for Melancholy*. Garden City, N.Y.: Doubleday, 1959.

————. *The October Country.* New York: Ballantine, 1955.

————. *R Is for Rocket.* Garden City, N.Y.: Doubleday, 1962.

————. *S Is for Space.* Garden City, N.Y.: Doubleday, 1966.

————. *The Stories of Ray Bradbury.* New York: Knopf, 1980.

————. *Twice Twenty-Two; The Golden Apples of the Sun; A Medicine for Melancholy.* Garden City, N.Y.: Doubleday, 1966.

————. *The Vintage Bradbury: Ray Bradbury's Own Selection of His Best Stories.* New York: Vintage, 1965.

Brodkey, Harold. *First Love and Other Sorrows.* New York: Dial, 1958.

Bromell, Henry. *I Know Your Heart, Marco Polo.* New York: Knopf, 1979.

————. *The Slightest Distance.* Boston: Houghton Mifflin, 1974.

Brophy, Brigid. *The Adventures of God in His Search for the Black Girl.* Boston: Little, Brown, 1974.

Brown, Rosellen, *Street Games.* New York: Doubleday, 1974.

Buck, Pearl S. *The Woman Who Was Changed and Other Stories.* New York: Crowell, 1979.

Bullins, Ed. *The Hungered One.* New York: Morrow, 1971.

Busch, Frederick. *Breathing Trouble.* London: Calder & Boyers, 1973.

————. *Domestic Particulars: A Family Chronicle.* New York: New Directions, 1976.

————. *Hardwater Country.* New York: Knopf, 1979.

Calisher, Hortense. *The Collected Stories of Hortense Calisher.* New York: Arbor House, 1975.

————. *Extreme Magic: A Novella, and Other Stories.* Boston: Little, Brown, 1964.

————. *In the Absence of Angels: Stories.* Boston: Little, Brown, 1964.

————. *Tale for the Mirror: A Novella and Other Stories.* Boston: Little, Brown, 1962.

Canzoneri, Robert. *Barbed Wire and Other Stories.* New York: Dial, 1970.

Capote, Truman. *Breakfast at Tiffany's: A Short Novel and Three Stories* New York: Random House, 1958.

————. *Music for Chameleons.* New York: Random House, 1980.

————. *A Tree of Night and Other Stories.* New York: Random House, 1949.

Carr, Pat. *The Women in the Mirror.* Iowa City: University of Iowa Press, 1977.

Carver, Raymond. *Furious Seasons.* Santa Barbara: Capra Press, 1977.

————. *Will You Please Be Quiet, Please?.* New York: McGraw-Hill, 1976.

Cassill, R. V. *The Father and Other Stories.* New York: Simon & Schuster, 1965.

————. *The Happy Marriage and Other Stories.* West Lafayette, Ind.: Purdue University Press, 1956.

Cheever, John. *The Brigadier and the Golf Widow.* New York: Harper & Row, 1964.

————. *The Enormous Radio and Other Stories.* New York: Funk & Wagnalls, 1953.

————. *The Housebreaker of Shady Hill and Other Stories.* New York: Harper, 1958.

————. *Some People, Places, and Things that Will Not Appear in My Next Novel.* New York: Harper, 1961.

————. *The Stories of John Cheever.* New York: Knopf, 1978.

————. *The Way Some People Live: A Book of Stories.* New York: Random House, 1943.

————. *The World of Apples.* New York: Knopf, 1973.

Chesnutt, Charles W. *The Wife of His Youth and Other Stories.* Ann Arbor: University of Michigan Press, 1968.
Clark, Eleanor. *Dr. Heart: A Novella and Other Stories.* New York: Pantheon, 1974.
Clark, Walter Van Tilburg. *The Watchful Gods and Other Stories.* New York: Random House, 1950.
Clayton, John Bell. *The Strangers Were There: Selected Stories.* New York: Macmillan, 1957.
Clearman, Mary. *Lambing Out.* Columbia: University of Missouri Press, 1977.
Coates, Robert M. *All the Year Round.* New York: Harcourt Brace, 1943.
———. *Hour After Westerly and Other Stories.* New York: Harcourt Brace, 1957.
———. *The Man Just Ahead of You.* New York: Sloane, 1964.
Collier, John. *Fancies and Goodnights.* Garden City, N.Y.: Doubleday, 1951.
———. *The John Collier Reader.* New York: Knopf, 1972.
Colter, Cyrus. *The Beach Umbrella.* Iowa City: University of Iowa Press, 1970.
Colwin, Laurie. *Passion and Affect.* New York: Viking, 1974.
Connell, Evan S. *The Anatomy Lesson and Other Stories.* New York: Viking, 1957.
———. *At the Crossroads: Stories.* New York: Simon & Schuster, 1965.
———. *Saint Augustine's Pigeon.* Berkeley, Calif.: North Point Press, 1980.
Coover, Robert. *Pricksongs and Descants.* New York: Dutton, 1969.
Corrington, John William. *The Actes and Monuments.* Urbana: University of Illinois Press, 1978.
———. *The Lonesome Traveler.* New York: Putnam's, 1968.
Costello, Mark. *The Murphy Stories.* Urbana: University of Illinois Press, 1973.
Cullinan, Elizabeth. *The Time of Adam.* New York: Houghton Mifflin, 1971.
———. *Yellow Roses.* New York: Viking, 1977.
Curley, Daniel. *In the Hands of Our Enemies.* Urbana: University of Illinois Press, 1970.
———. *Love in the Winter.* Urbana: University of Illinois Press, 1976.
———. *That Marriage Bed of Procrustes.* Boston: Beacon, 1957.
Davenport, Guy. *Da Vinci's Bicycle: Ten Stories.* Baltimore: Johns Hopkins University Press, 1979.
———. *Tatlin! Six Stories.* New York: Scribner's, 1974.
Davis, Olivia. *The Scent of Apples.* Boston: Houghton Mifflin, 1972.
Dawkins, Cecil. *The Quiet Enemy.* New York: Atheneum, 1963.
Dawson, Fielding. *The Man Who Changed Overnight and Other Stories and Dreams.* Santa Barbara: Black Sparrow, 1976.
Dixon, Stephen. *14 Stories.* Baltimore: Johns Hopkins University Press, 1980.
Dubus, Andre. *Adultery and Other Choices.* Boston: Godine, 1977.
———. *Finding a Girl in America: Ten Stories and a Novella.* Boston: Godine, 1980.
———. *Separate Flights.* Boston: Godine, 1975.
Dumas, Henry. *Ark of Bones and Other Stories.* New York: Random House, 1974.
———. *Rope of Wind and Other Stories.* New York: Random House, 1979.
Dubek, Stuart. *Childhood and Other Neighborhoods.* New York: Viking, 1980.
Elkin, Stanley. *Criers and Kibitzers, Kibitzers and Criers.* New York: Random House, 1966.

————. *The Living End.* New York: Dutton, 1979.

————. *Searches and Seizures.* New York: Random House, 1973.

————. *Stanley Elkin's Greatest Hits.* New York: Dutton, 1980.

Elliott, George P. *Among the Dangs: Ten Short Stories.* New York: Holt, 1961.

————. *An Hour of Last Things and Other Stories.* New York: Harper & Row, 1968.

Enright, Elizabeth. *Borrowed Summer and Other Stories.* New York: Rinehart, 1946.

————. *Doublefields: Memories and Stories.* New York: Harcourt Brace, 1966.

————. *The Moment Before the Rain.* New York: Harcourt Brace, 1955.

————. *The Riddle of the Fly and Other Stories.* New York: Harcourt Brace, 1959.

Epstein, Leslie. *The Steinway Quintet Plus Four.* Boston: Little, Brown, 1976.

Epstein, Seymour. *A Penny for Charity.* Boston: Little, Brown, 1965.

Farrell, James T. *American Dream Girl.* New York: Vanguard, 1950.

————. *Childhood Is Not Forever.* Garden City, N.Y.: Doubleday, 1969.

————. *A Dangerous Woman and Other Stories.* New York: Vanguard, 1957.

————. *French Girls Are Vicious and Other Stories.* New York: Vanguard, 1955.

————. *Further Short Stories.* Garden City, N.Y.: Sun Dial, 1948.

————. *Judith and Other Stories.* Garden City, N.Y.: Doubleday, 1973.

————. *The Life Adventurous and Other Stories.* New York: Vanguard, 1947.

————. *Olive and Mary Anne.* New York: Stonehill, 1977.

————. *Omnibus of Short Stories.* New York: Vanguard, 1956.

————. *Short Stories.* New York: Vanguard, 1951.

Faulkner, William. *The Collected Stories of William Faulkner.* New York: Random House, 1950.

————. *Knight's Gambit.* New York: Random House, 1949.

————. *Uncollected Stories of William Faulkner.* New York: Random House, 1979.

Faust, Irvin. *Roar Lion Roar and Other Stories.* New York: Random House, 1964.

Fetler, Andrew. *To Byzantium.* Urbana: University of Illinois Press, 1976.

Fetler, James. *Impossible Appetites.* Iowa City: University of Iowa Press, 1980.

Fitzgerald, F. Scott. *The Price Was High: The Last Uncollected Stories of F. Scott Fitzgerald.* New York: Harcourt Brace Jovanovich, 1979.

Francis, H. E. *The Itinerary of Beggars.* Iowa City: University of Iowa Press, 1973.

————. *Naming Things.* Urbana: University of Illinois Press, 1980.

Friedman, Bruce Jay. *Black Angels: Stories.* New York: Simon & Schuster, 1966.

————. *Far from the City of Class and Other Stories.* New York: Frommer-Pasmantier, 1963.

Friedman, Paul. *And If Defeated Allege Fraud.* Urbana: University of Illinois Press, 1971.

Gaines, Ernest J. *Bloodlines.* New York: Dial, 1968.

Gallant, Mavis. *From the Fifteenth District.* New York: Random House, 1979.

Gardner, John. *The King's Indian: Stories and Tales.* New York: Knopf, 1974.

Garrett, George P. *Cold Ground Was My Bed Last Night.* Columbia: University of Missouri Press, 1964.

————. *In the Briar Patch: A Book of Stories.* Austin: University of Texas Press, 1961.

————. *King of the Mountain.* New York: Scribner's, 1957.

———. *The Magic Striptease.* Garden City, N.Y.: Doubleday, 1973.

Gass, William H. *In the Heart of the Heart of the Country and Other Stories.* New York: Harper & Row, 1968.

———. *Willie Masters' Lonesome Wife.* New York: Knopf, 1971.

Gellhorn, Martha. *The Honeyed Place: Stories.* Garden City, N. Y.: Doubleday, 1953.

———. *Pretty Tales for Tired People.* New York: Simon & Schuster, 1965.

———. *Two By Two.* New York: Simon & Schuster, 1958.

Gill, Brendan. *Ways Of Loving.* New York: Harcourt Brace Jovanovich, 1974.

Godwin, Gail. *Dream Children.* Knopf: New York, 1976.

Gold, Herbert. *Love and Like.* New York: Dial, 1960.

———. *The Magic Will: Stories and Essays of a Decade.* New York: Random House, 1971.

Goldberg, Gerald Jay. *A Hundred Twenty-Six Days of Continuous Sunshine.* New York: Dial, 1972.

Goldberg, Lester. *One More River.* Urbana: University of Illinois Press, 1977.

Gordon, Caroline. *The Forest of the South.* New York: Scribner's, 1945.

———. *Old Red and Other Stories.* New York: Scribner's, 1963.

Goyen, William. *The Collected Stories of William Goyen.* Garden City, N.Y.: Doubleday, 1975.

———. *The Faces of Blood Kindred: A Novella and Ten Stories.* New York: Random House, 1960.

———. *Ghost and Flesh: Stories and Tales.* New York: Random House, 1952.

———. *Selected Writings of William Goyen: Eight Favorites by a Master American Storyteller.* New York: Random House, 1974.

Grau, Shirley Ann. *The Black Prince and Other Stories.* New York: Knopf, 1954.

———. *The Wind Shifting West.* New York: Knopf, 1973.

Greenberg, Alvin. *The Discovery of America and Other Tales of Terror and Self-Exploration.* Baton Rouge: Louisiana State University Press, 1980.

Greenberg, Joanne. *High Crimes and Misdemeanors.* New York: Holt, Rinehart & Winston, 1980.

———. *Rites of Passage.* New York: Holt, Rinehart & Winston, 1972.

Hale, Nancy. *Between the Dark and the Daylight.* New York: Scribner's, 1943.

———. *The Empress's Ring.* New York: Scribner's, 1955.

———. *The Pattern of Perfection: Thirteen Stories.* Boston: Little, Brown, 1960.

Hall, James B. *Fifteen by Three.* New York: New Directions, 1957.

———. *The Short Hall: New and Selected Stories.* Denver: Stonehenge Books, 1980.

———. *Us He Devours.* New York: New Directions, 1964.

Hannah, Barry. *Airships.* New York: Knopf, 1978.

Harnack, Curtis. *Under My Wings Everything Prospers.* New York: Doubleday, 1977.

Harrison, William. *Roller Ball Murder.* New York: Morrow, 1974.

Hawkes, John. *Lunar Landscapes.* New York: New Directions, 1969.

Hedin, Mary. *Fly Away Home.* Iowa City: University of Iowa Press, 1979.

Helprin, Mark. *A Dove of the East and Other Stories.* New York: Knopf, 1975.

Hemenway, Robert. *The Girl Who Sang With the Beatles.* New York: Knopf, 1970.

Henson, Robert. *Transports and Disgraces.* Urbana: University of Illinois Press, 1980.

Hermann, John. *An Agreement Between Us.* Columbia: University of Missouri Press, 1972.

Himes, Chester. *Black on Black: Baby Sister and Selected Writings.* New York: Doubleday, 1973.

Hoffman, William. *Virginia Reels.* Urbana: University of Illinois Press, 1978.

Huddle, David. *A Dream With No Stump Roots in It.* Columbia: University of Missouri Press, 1975.

Hughes, Langston. *The Best of Simple.* New York: Hill & Wang, 1961.

———. *The Langston Hughes Reader.* New York: Braziller, 1965.

———. *Laughing to Keep from Crying.* New York: Holt, Rinehart, 1952.

———. *Simple's Uncle Sam.* New York: Hill & Wang, 1965.

———. *Something in Common and Other Stories.* New York: Hill & Wang, 1963.

Hughes, Mary Gray. *The Calling.* Urbana: University of Illinois Press, 1980.

Humphrey, William. *The Last Husband and Other Stories.* New York: Morrow, 1953.

———. *A Time and a Place: Stories of the Red River Country.* New York: Knopf, 1968.

Jackson, Charles. *Earthly Creatures: Ten Stories.* New York: Farrar, Straus, 1953.

———. *The Sunnier Side: Twelve Arcadian Tales.* New York: Farrar, Straus, 1950.

Jackson, Shirley. *Come Along With Me: Part of a Novel, Sixteen Stories and Three Lectures.* New York: Viking, 1968.

———. *The Lottery: or, The Adventures of James Harris.* New York: Farrar, Straus, 1949.

———. *The Magic of Shirley Jackson.* New York: Farrar, Straus & Giroux, 1966.

Jacobsen, Josephine. *A Walk with Raschid and Other Stories.* Winston-Salem, N.C.: Jackpine Press, 1978.

Johnson, Josephine. *The Sorcerer's Son and Other Stories.* New York: Simon & Schuster, 1965.

Jones, Ann. *Hope Should Always.* Columbia: University of Missouri Press, 1973.

Jones, Gayl. *White Rat.* New York: Random House, 1977.

Just, Ward. *The Congressman Who Loved Flaubert and Other Washington Stories.* Boston: Little, Brown, 1973.

———. *Honor, Power, Riches, Fame, and the Love of Women.* New York: Dutton, 1979.

Kavaler, Rebecca. *The Further Adventures of Brunhild.* Columbia: University of Missouri Press, 1978.

Kentfield, Calvin. *The Angel and the Sailor: A Novella and Nine Stories.* New York: McGraw-Hill, 1957.

———. *The Great Wandering Goony Bird: Ten Short Stories.* New York: Random House, 1963.

Kim, Yong Ik. *Love in Winter.* New York: Doubleday, 1969.

Knowles, John. *Phineas: Six Stories.* New York: Random House, 1968.

Kranes, David. *Hunters in the Snow.* Salt Lake City: University of Utah Press, 1979.

LaFarge, Oliver. *All the Young Men.* Boston: Houghton Mifflin, 1949.

———. *The Door in the Wall: Stories.* Boston: Houghton Mifflin, 1965.

———. *Pause in the Desert: A Collection of Short Stories.* Boston: Houghton Mifflin, 1957.

LaSalle, Peter. *The Graves of Famous Writers and Other Stories.* Columbia: University of Missouri Press, 1980.

Lowry, Robert. *Happy New Year, Kamerades!* Garden City, N.Y.: Doubleday, 1954.

————. *The Last Party: A Memorable Collection of Short Stories.* New York: Popular Library, 1965.

————. *New York Call Girl.* Garden City, N.Y.: Doubleday, 1958.

————. *Party of Dreamers.* New York: Fleet, 1962.

————. *The Wolf that Fed Us.* Garden City, N.Y.: Doubleday, 1949.

MacMillan, Ian. *Light and Power.* Columbia. University of Missouri Press, 1980.

Madden, David. *The Shadow Knows.* Baton Rouge: Louisiana State University Press, 1970.

Malamud, Bernard. *Idiots First.* New York: Farrar, Straus, 1963.

————. *The Magic Barrel.* New York: Farrar, Straus, 1958.

————. *A Malamud Reader.* New York: Farrar, Straus & Giroux, 1967.

————. *Rembrandt's Hat.* New York: Farrar, Straus & Giroux, 1973.

Marsh, Willard. *Beachhead in Bohemia.* Baton Rouge: Louisiana State University Press, 1970.

Matthews, Jack. *Bitter Knowledge.* New York: Scribner's, 1964.

————. *Dubious Persuasions.* Baltimore: Johns Hopkins University Press, 1980.

McCarthy, Mary. *Cast a Cold Eye.* New York: Harcourt Brace, 1950.

McCullers, Carson. *The Ballad of the Sad Cafe: The Novels and Stories of Carson McCullers.* Boston: Houghton Mifflin, 1951.

————. *The Mortgaged Heart.* Boston: Houghton Mifflin, 1971.

McNulty, John. *A Man Gets Around.* Boston: Little, Brown, 1951.

————. *Third Avenue, New York.* Boston: Little, Brown, 1946.

————. *The World of John McNulty.* Garden City, N.Y.: Doubleday, 1957.

McPherson, James Alan. *Elbow Room.* Boston: Little, Brown, 1977.

————. *Hue and Cry.* Boston: Little, Brown, 1969.

Michaels, Leonard. *Going Places.* New York: Farrar, Straus & Giroux, 1969.

————. *I Would Have Saved Them If I Could.* New York: Farrar, Straus & Giroux, 1975.

Michener, James A. *Return to Paradise.* New York: Random House, 1951.

————. *Tales of the South Pacific.* New York: Macmillan, 1950.

Mills, William. *I Know a Place.* Baton Rouge: Press of the Nightowl, 1976.

Minot, Stephen. *Crossings.* Urbana: University of Illinois Press, 1975.

Morgan, Berry. *The Mystic Adventures of Roxy Stoner.* Boston: Houghton Mifflin, 1974.

Morgan, Speer. *Frog Gig and Other Stories.* Columbia: University of Missouri Press, 1976.

Morris, Mary. *Vanishing Animals and Other Stories.* Boston: Godine, 1979.

Morris, Wright. *Green Grass, Blue Sky, White House.* Los Angeles: Black Sparrow, 1970.

————. *Here Is Einbaum.* Los Angeles: Black Sparrow, 1973.

————. *Real Losses, Imaginary Gains.* New York: Harper & Row, 1976.

Munro, Alice. *The Beggar Mind.* New York: Knopf, 1979.

————. *Something I've Been Meaning to Tell You.* New York: McGraw-Hill, 1974.

Nabokov, Vladimir. *Details of a Sunset and Other Stories.* New York: McGraw-Hill, 1976.

————. *Nabokov's Congeries.* New York: Viking, 1968.

————. *Nabokov's Dozen: A Collection of Thirteen Stories.* Garden City, N.Y.: Doubleday, 1958.

————. *Nabokov's Quartet.* New York: Phaedra, 1966.

————. *Nine Stories.* New York: New Directions, 1947.

————. *A Russian Beauty and Other Stories.* New York: McGraw-Hill, 1973.

————. *Tyrants Destroyed and Other Stories.* New York: McGraw-Hill, 1975.

Nelson, Kent. *The Tennis Player.* Urbana: University of Illinois Press, 1977.

Nelson, Richard K. *Shadow of the Hunter.* Chicago: University of Chicago Press, 1980.

Nemerov, Howard. *A Commodity of Dreams and Other Stories.* New York: Simon & Schuster, 1959.

————. *Stories, Fables and Other Diversions.* Boston: Godine, 1971.

Neugeboren, Jay. *Corky's Brother.* New York: Farrar, Straus & Giroux, 1969.

Newhouse, Edward. *Anything Can Happen.* New York: Harcourt Brace, 1941.

————. *The Iron Chain.* New York: Harcourt Brace, 1946.

————. *Many Are Called: Forty-Two Short Stories.* New York: Sloane, 1951.

Nissenson, Hugh. *In the Reign of Peace.* New York: Farrar, Straus & Giroux, 1972.

————. *A Pile of Stones: Short Stories.* New York: Scribner's, 1965.

Oates, Joyce Carol. *All the Good People I've Left Behind.* Santa Barabara: Black Sparrow, 1979.

————. *By the North Gate.* New York: Vanguard, 1963.

————. *Crossing the Border: Fifteen Tales.* New York: Vanguard, 1976.

————. *The Goddess and Other Women.* New York: Vanguard, 1974.

————. *The Hungry Ghosts: Seven Allusive Comedies.* Santa Barbara: Black Sparrow, 1974.

————. *Marriages and Infidelities: Short Stories.* New York: Vanguard, 1972.

————. *Night-Side: Eighteen Tales.* New York: Vanguard, 1977.

Oates, Joyce Carol, and Fernandes. *The Poisoned Kiss, and Other Stories from the Portuguese.* New York: Vanguard, 1975.

Oates, Joyce Carol. *The Seduction, and Other Stories.* Santa Barbara: Black Sparrow, 1975.

————. *Upon the Sweeping Flood and Other Stories.* New York: Vanguard, 1966.

————. *The Wheel of Love and Other Stories.* New York: Vanguard, 1970.

————. *Where Are You Going, Where Have You Been? Stories of Young America.* New York: Fawcett, 1974.

O'Connor, Flannery. *The Complete Stories.* New York: Farrar, Straus & Giroux, 1971.

————. *Everything That Rises Must Converge.* New York: Farrar, Straus & Giroux, 1965.

————. *A Good Man is Hard to Find and Other Stories.* New York: Harcourt Brace, 1955.

O'Connor, Philip F. *Old Morals, Small Continents, Darker Times.* Iowa City: University of Iowa Press, 1971.

————. *A Season for Unnatural Causes.* Urbana: University of Illinois Press, 1975.

O'Hara, John. *And Other Stories.* New York: Random House, 1968.

————. *Assembly.* New York: Random House, 1961.

————. *The Cape Cod Lighter.* New York: Random House, 1962.

————. *49 Stories.* New York: Modern Library, 1963.

————. *The Good Samaritan and Other Stories.* New York: Random House, 1974.

————. *The Hat on the Bed.* New York: Random House, 1963.

————. *Hellbox.* New York: Random House, 1947.

————. *Here's O'Hara: Three Novels and Twenty Short Stories.* New York: Duell, Sloan, and Pearce, 1946.

————. *The Horse Knows the Way.* New York: Random House, 1964.

————. *The O'Hara Generation.* New York: Random House, 1969.

————. *Pipe Night.* New York: Duell, Sloan, and Pearce, 1945.

————. *Selected Short Stories.* New York: Modern Library, 1956.

————. *The Time Element and Other Stories.* New York: Random House, 1972.

————. *Waiting for Winter.* New York: Random House, 1966.

Olsen, Tillie. *Tell Me a Riddle: A Collection.* Philadelphia: Lippincott, 1961.

Osborn, Carolyn. *A Horse of Another Color.* Urbana: University of Illinois Press, 1977.

Otto, Lon. *A Nest of Hooks.* Iowa City: University of Iowa Press, 1978.

Ozick, Cynthia. *Bloodshed and Three Novellas.* New York: Knopf, 1976.

————. *The Pagan Rabbi and Other Stories.* New York: Knopf, 1971.

Paley, Grace. *Enormous Changes at the Last Minute: Stories.* New York: Farrar, Straus & Giroux, 1974.

————. *The Little Disturbances of Man.* Garden City, N.Y.: Doubleday, 1959.

Peden, William Harwood. *Night in Funland and Other Stories.* Baton Rouge: Louisiana State University Press, 1968.

Peterkin, Julia. *Collected Short Stories of Julia Peterkin.* Columbia: University of South Carolina Press, 1970.

Petesch, Natalie L. M. *After the First Death, There Is No Other.* Iowa City: University of Iowa Press, 1974.

Petrakis, Harry Mark. *Pericles on 31st Street.* Chicago: Quadrangle, 1965.

————. *The Waves of Night.* New York: McKay, 1969.

Petry, Ann. *Miss Muriel and Other Stories.* Boston: Houghton Mifflin, 1971.

Phillips, Jayne Ann. *Black Tickets.* New York: Delacorte, 1979.

Phillips, Robert. *The Land of Lost Content.* New York: Vanguard, 1970.

Poverman, C. E. *The Black Velvet Girl.* Iowa City: University of Iowa Press, 1976.

Powers, J. F. *Look How the Fish Live.* New York: Knopf, 1975.

————. *The Presence of Grace.* Garden City, N.Y.: Doubleday, 1956.

————. *Prince of Darkness and Other Stories.* Garden City, N.Y.: Doubleday, 1947.

Price, Reynolds. *The Names and Faces of Heroes.* New York: Atheneum, 1963.

————. *Permanent Errors.* New York: Atheneum, 1970.

Purdy, James. *Children Is All.* New York: New Directions, 1962.

————. *Color of Darkness: Eleven Stories and a Novella.* New York: New Directions, 1957.

Ritcher, Conrad. *The Rawhide Knot and Other Stories.* New York: Knopf, 1978.

Rogin, Gilbert. *The Fencing Master and Other Stories.* New York: Random House, 1965.

Rooke, Leon. *Last One Home Sleeps in the Yellow Bed.* Baton Rouge: Louisiana State University Press, 1968.

Rosten, Leo. *The Many Worlds of L*e*o R*o*s*t*e*n.* New York: Harper & Row, 1964.

————. *The Return of H*y*m*a*n K*a*p*l*a*n.* New York: Harper & Row, 1959.

Roth, Philip. *Goodbye, Columbus and Five Short Stories.* Boston: Houghton Mifflin, 1959.

————. *My Life As a Man.* New York: Holt, 1974.

Salinger, J. D. *Franny and Zooey.* Boston: Little, Brown, 1961.

————. *Nine Stories.* Boston: Little, Brown, 1953.

————. *Raise High the Roof Beam, Carpenters, and Seymour: An Introduction.* Boston: Little, Brown, 1963.

Saroyan, William. *The Assyrian and Other Stories.* New York: Harcourt Brace, 1950.

————. *Love.* New York: Lion, 1955.

————. *The Man with His Heart in the Highlands and Other Stories.* New York: Dell, 1968.

————. *A Saroyan Special: Selected Short Stories.* New York: Harcourt Brace, 1948.

————. *The William Saroyan Reader.* New York: Braziller, 1958.

————. *The Whole Voyald and Other Stories.* Boston: Little, Brown, 1956.

Schaeffer, Susan Fromberg. *The Queen of Egypt.* New York: Dutton, 1980.

Sayles, John. *The Anarchists' Convention.* Boston: Little, Brown, 1979.

Schorer, Mark, and August Derleth. *Colonel Markesan and Less Pleasant People.* Sauk City, Wis.: Arkham House, 1966.

Schorer, Mark. *Pieces of Life.* New York: Farrar, Straus & Giroux, 1977.

————. *The State of Mind.* Boston: Houghton Mifflin, 1947.

Schott, Max. *Up Where I Used to Live.* Urbana: University of Illinois Press, 1978.

Schwartz, Delmore. *In Dreams Begin Responsibilities and Other Stories.* New York: New Directions, 1978.

————. *The World Is a Wedding.* New York: New Directions, 1948.

Shaw, Irwin. *Act of Faith and Other Stories.* New York: Random House, 1946.

————. *God Was Here But He Left Early: Short Fiction.* New York: Arbor House, 1973.

————. *Love on a Dark Street and Other Stories.* New York: Delacorte, 1965.

————. *Selected Short Stories of Irwin Shaw.* New York: Modern Library, 1961.

————. *Short Stories: Five Decades.* New York: Delacorte, 1978.

————. *Tip On a Dead Jockey and Other Stories.* New York: Random House, 1957.

Schelnutt, Eve. *The Love Child.* Santa Barbara: Black Sparrow, 1979.

Sherwin, Judith Johnson. *The Life of Riot.* New York: Atheneum, 1970.

Singer, Isaac Bashevis. *A Crown of Feathers and Other Stories.* New York: Farrar, Straus & Giroux, 1973.

————. *A Day of Pleasures.* New York: Farrar, Straus & Giroux, 1969.

————. *A Friend of Kafka and Other Stories.* New York: Farrar, Straus & Giroux, 1970.

————. *Gimpel the Fool and Other Stories.* New York: Noonday, 1957.

————. *An Isaac Bashevis Singer Reader.* New York: Farrar, Straus & Giroux, 1971.

————. *Old Love.* New York: Farrar, Straus & Giroux, 1979.

————. *Passions and Other Stories.* New York: Farrar, Straus & Giroux, 1975.

————. *The Seance and Other Stories.* New York: Farrar, Straus & Giroux, 1975.

————. *Selected Short Stories of Isaac Bashevis Singer.* New York: Modern Library, 1966.

————. *Short Friday and Other Stories.* New York: Farrar, Straus, 1964.

————. *The Spinoza of Market Street.* New York: Farrar, Straus, 1961.

————. *When Schlemiel Went to Warsaw and Other Stories.* New York: Farrar, Straus & Giroux, 1968.

————. *Zlateh the Goat and Other Stories.* New York: Harper & Row, 1966.

Sontag, Susan. *I, Etcetera.* New York: Farrar, Straus & Giroux, 1978.
Southern, Terry. *Red Dirt Marijuana and Other Tastes.* New York: New American Library, 1967.
Spencer, Elizabeth. *Ship Island and Other Stories.* New York: McGraw-Hill, 1968.
Stafford, Jean. *Bad Characters.* New York: Farrar, Straus, 1964.
————. *Children Are Bored on Sunday.* New York: Harcourt Brace, 1953.
————. *The Collected Stories of Jean Stafford.* New York: Farrar, Straus & Giroux, 1969.
Steele, Max. *When She Brushed Her Hair and Other Stories.* New York: Harper & Row, 1968.
Stegner, Wallace. *The City of the Living and Other Stories.* Boston: Houghton Mifflin, 1956.
————. *The Women On the Wall.* Boston: Houghton Mifflin, 1950.
Stern, Richard. *1968.* New York: Holt, Rinehart & Winston, 1970.
————. *Packages.* New York: Coward, McCann & Geoghegan, 1980.
Stewart, John. *Curving Road.* Urbana: University of Illinois Press, 1975.
Stuart, Jesse. *Clearing the Sky and Other Stories.* New York: McGraw-Hill, 1950.
————. *Come Back to the Farm.* New York: McGraw-Hill, 1971.
————. *Come Gentle Spring.* New York: McGraw-Hill, 1969.
————. *Dawn of Remembered Spring.* New York: McGraw-Hill, 1972
————. *A Jesse Stuart Harvest.* New York: Dell, 1965.
————. *A Jesse Stuart Reader.* New York: McGraw-Hill, 1963.
————. *My Land Has a Voice.* New York: McGraw-Hill, 1966.
————. *Plowshare in Heaven: Stories.* New York: McGraw-Hill, 1958.
————. *Save Every Lamb.* New York: McGraw-Hill, 1964.
————. *Tales from the Plum Grove Hills.* New York: Dutton, 1946.
————. *32 Votes Before Breakfast: Politics at the Grass Roots as Seen in Short Stories.* New York: McGraw-Hill, 1974.
Styron, William. *The Long March.* New York: Random House, 1956.
Sukenick, Ronald. *The Death of the Novel and Other Stories.* New York: Dial, 1969.
Summers, Hollis. *How They Chose the Dead.* Baton Rouge: Louisiana State University Press, 1973.
Swan, Gladys. *On the Edge of the Desert.* Urbana: University of Illinois Press, 1979.
Targan, Barry. *Harry Belten and the Mendelssohn Violin Concerto.* Iowa City: University of Iowa Press, 1975.
————. *Surviving Adverse Seasons.* Urbana: University of Illinois Press, 1979.
Taylor, Harry H. *The Man Who Tried Out for Tarzan.* Baton Rouge: Louisiana State University Press, 1973.
Taylor, Peter. *The Collected Stories of Peter Taylor.* New York: Farrar, Straus & Giroux, 1969.
————. *Happy Families Are All Alike: A Collection of Stories.* New York: McDowell, Obolensky, 1959.
————. *In the Miro District and Other Stories.* New York: Knopf, 1977.
————. *A Long Fourth and Other Stories.* New York: Harcourt Brace, 1948.

————. *Miss Leonara When Last Seen and Fifteen Other Stories.* New York: Obolensky, 1963.

————. *The Widows of Thornton.* New York: Harcourt Brace, 1954.

Theroux, Paul. *Sinning With Annie and Other Stories.* Boston: Houghton Mifflin, 1972.

————. *World's End and Other Stories.* Boston: Houghton Mifflin, 1980.

Thompson, Jean. *The Gasoline Wars.* Urbana: University of Illinois Press, 1979.

Traven, B. *The Kidnapped Saint and Other Stories.* New York: Lawrence Hill, 1975.

————. *The Night Visitor and Other Stories.* New York: Hill & Wang, 1966.

Updike, John. *Bech: A Book.* New York: Knopf, 1970.

————. *Museums and Women and Other Stories.* New York: Knopf, 1972.

————. *The Music School: Short Stories.* New York: Knopf, 1966.

————. *Olinger Stories: A Selection.* New York: Vintage, 1964.

————. *Pigeon Feathers, and Other Stories.* New York: Knopf, 1962.

————. *Problems, and Other Stories.* New York: Knopf, 1979.

————. *The Same Door: Short Stories.* New York: Knopf, 1959.

————. *Too Far To Go: The Maples Stories.* New York: Fawcett, 1979.

Van Doren, Mark. *Collected Stories.* New York: Hill & Wang, 1962.

————. *Collected Stories.* Vols. II & III. New York: Hill & Wang, 1965.

————. *Home With Hazel and Other Stories.* New York: Harcourt Brace, 1957.

————. *Nobody Said a Word and Other Stories.* New York: Holt, 1953.

————. *Short Stories.* New York: Abelard-Schumann, 1950.

Vonnegut, Kurt, Jr. *Welcome To The Monkey House.* New York: Delacorte, 1968.

Walker, Alice. *In Love and Trouble: Stories of Black Women.* New York: Harcourt Brace Jovanovich, 1973.

Warren, Robert Penn. *The Circus in the Attic and Other Stories.* New York: Harcourt Brace, 1948.

Weaver, Gordon. *The Entombed Man of Thule.* Baton Rouge: Louisiana State University Press, 1972.

————. *Getting Serious.* Baton Rouge: Louisiana State University Press, 1980.

————. *Such Waltzing Was Not Easy.* Urbana: University of Illinois Press, 1975.

Weidman, Jerome. *The Captain's Tiger.* New York: Reynal, 1947.

————. *The Death of Dickie Draper and Nine Other Stories.* New York: Random House, 1965.

————. *My Father Sits in the Dark and Other Selected Stories.* New York: Random House, 1961.

Welty, Eudora. *The Bride of the Innisfallen and Other Stories.* New York: Harcourt Brace, 1955.

————. *The Collected Stories of Eudora Welty.* New York: Harcourt Brace Jovanovich, 1980.

————. *Curtain of Green.* Garden City, N.Y.: Doubleday, 1941.

————. *The Golden Apples.* New York: Harcourt Brace, 1949.

————. *The Ponder Heart.* New York: Harcourt Brace, 1954.

————. *Selected Stories.* New York: Modern Library, 1954.

————. *The Wide Net and Other Stories.* New York: Harcourt Brace, 1953.

West, Jessamyn. *Crimson Ramblers of the World, Farewell.* New York: Harcourt Brace Jovanovich, 1970.

————. *Except for Me and Thee: A Companion to the Friendly Persuasion.* New York: Harcourt Brace, 1969.

————. *The Friendly Persuasion.* New York: Harcourt Brace, 1945.

————. *Love, Death, and the Ladies' Drill Team.* New York: Harcourt Brace, 1955.

Wier, Allen. *Things About to Disappear.* Baton Rouge: Louisiana State University Press, 1978.

Williams, Tennessee. *Eight Mortal Ladies Possessed: A Book of Stories.* New York: New Directions, 1974.

————. *Hard Candy: A Book of Stories.* New York: New Directions, 1954.

————. *The Knightly Quest: A Novella and Four Short Stories.* New York: New Directions, 1967.

————. *One Arm and Other Stories.* New York: New Directions, 1954.

Wilson, Robley, Jr. *The Pleasures of Manhood.* Urbana: University of Illinois Press, 1977.

Windham, Donald. *Emblems of Conduct.* New York: Scribner's, 1963.

————. *The Warm Country.* New York: Scribner's, 1962.

Yates, Richard. *Eleven Kinds of Loneliness: Short Stories.* Boston: Little, Brown, 1962.

Wright, Richard. *Eight Men.* Cleveland: World, 1961.

Zacharias, Lee. *Helping Muriel Make It Through the Night.* Baton Rouge: Louisiana State University Press, 1975.

Zelver, Patricia. *The Man of Middle Age and Other Stories.* New York: Holt Rinehart & Winston, 1980.

Selected Bibliography of
Articles of General Interest

Baldeshwiler, Eileen. "The Lyric Short Story: The Sketch of a History." *Studies in Short Fiction* 6, no. 4 (1969): 443—53. Traces its evolution from Turgenev through Welty and Updike.

Fitz Gerald, Gregory. "The Satiric Short Story: A Definition." *Studies in Short Fiction* 5, no. 4 (1968): 349—54. Includes well-chosen examples to illustrate the author's rather precise assertions.

Friedman, Melvin J. "Dislocations of Setting and Word: Notes on American Fiction Since 1950." *Studies in American Fiction* 5, no. 1 (1977): 79—98. Covers most authors in this book, viewing their relationships to contemporary aesthetics.

Friedman, Norman. "What Makes a Short Story Short?" *Modern Fiction Studies* 4, no. 2 (1958): 103—117. Uses object and manner for its criteria.

Galloway, David D. "Clown and Saint: The Hero in Current American Fiction." *Critique* 7, no. 3 (1965): 46—64. Includes discussion of Bellow, Elkin, and Updike.

Gibaldi, Joseph. "Towards a Definition of the Novella." *Studies in Short Fiction* 12, no. 2 (1975): 91—98. Uses mostly Renaissance examples to define this genre.

Gullason, Thomas A. "Revelation and Evolution: A Neglected Dimension of the Short Story." *Studies in Short Fiction* 10, no. 4 (1973): 347—56. Takes issue with Mark Schorer's idea of the short story as "moral revelation."

———. "The Short Story: An Underrated Art." *Studies in Short Fiction* 2, no. 1 (1964): 13—31. Another attempt to define the short story.

Hansen, Arlen J. "The Celebration of Solipsism: A New Trend in American Fiction." *Modern Fiction Studies* 14, no. 1 (1973): 5—16. Includes discussion of Vonnegut, Barthelme, and Gass.

May, Charles E. "The Unique Effect of the Short Story: A Reconsideration and an Example." *Studies in Short Fiction* 13, no. 3 (1976): 289—98. The short story is "primarily a literary mode that embodies and recapitulates mythic perception itself."

Olderman, Raymond M. "American Fiction 1974—1976: The People Who Fell to Earth." *Contemporary Literature* 19, no. 4 (1978): 497—527. A conveniently categorized, wide-ranging summary of the state of fiction in the mid-1970s.

Spilka, Mark. "The Necessary Stylist: A New Critical Revision." *Modern Fiction Studies* 6, no. 4 (1960—61): 283—97. Discusses the relationship between objectivity and style.

Selected Bibliography of
Books of General Interest

Aldridge, John W. *In Search of Heresy: American Literature in an Age of Conformity.* New York: McGraw-Hill, 1956. A collection of essays concerning affirmation and rejection of traditional moral values in contemporary fiction.

Balakian, Nona, and Simmons, Charles, eds. *The Creative Present: Notes on Contemporary American Fiction.* Garden City, N.Y.: Doubleday, 1963. Contains essays on Baldwin, Nabokov, Salinger, Bellow, Updike, Welty, Malamud, McCullers, and others.

Bates, H. E. *The Modern Short Story: A Critical Survey.* Boston: The Writer, 1972. Using mostly European examples, this volume is a historical survey beginning with Gogol and Poe.

Bruck, Peter. *The Black American Short Story in the 20th Century.* Amsterdam: B. R. Gruner, 1977. Essays on Hughes, Gaines, Baldwin, and others.

Core, George, ed. *Southern Fiction Today: Renascence and Beyond.* Athens: University of Georgia Press, 1969. Five essays on contemporary Southern fiction.

Current-Garcia, Eugene, and Patrick, Walton R. *What Is the Short Story?* Chicago: Scott, Foresman, 1961.

Finkelstein, Sidney. *Existentialism and Alienation in American Literature.* New York: International Publishers, 1965. Discusses the origins of existentialism and its relationship to Styron, Salinger, Updike, Mailer, Bellow, and Baldwin.

Gardner, John. *On Moral Fiction.* New York: Basic Books, 1978.

Gass, William H. *Fiction and the Figures of Life.* New York: Knopf, 1970. Includes discussion of Nabokov, Barthelme, Singer, and Updike, and an excellent section entitled "The Concept of Character in Fiction."

Graff, Gerald. *Literature Against Itself: Literary Ideas in Modern Society.* Chicago: University of Chicago Press, 1979.

Harper, Howard M., Jr. *Desperate Faith: A Study of Bellow, Salinger, Mailer, Baldwin, and Updike.* Chapel Hill: University of North Carolina Press, 1968. Finds parallels among these authors' view of the human condition.

Hendin, Josephine. *Vulnerable People: A View of American Fiction Since 1945.* New York: Oxford University Press, 1978. Contains interesting discussions of Barth, Bellow, Capote, Oates, O'Connor, Updike, and others, emphasizing real-world application of these writers' views.

Klinkowitz, Jerome. *The Practice of Fiction in America. Writers from Hawthorne to the Present.* Ames: Iowa State University Press, 1980.

Kumar, Shiv K, and McKean, Keith, eds. *Critical Approaches to Fiction.* New York: McGraw-Hill, 1968. Twenty-six diverse essays on the components of fiction and critical approaches—includes Bellow, Mary McCarthy, Welty, Mark Schorer, Philip Rahv, Wayne C. Booth, George P. Elliott, and more.

Lesser, Simon O. *Fiction and the Unconscious.* Boston: Beacon, 1957. Surveys the relationship between literature and psychology.

May, Charles E., ed. *Short Story Theories.* Athens: Ohio University Press, 1976. Twenty-four diverse selections and a valuable bibliography.

O'Connor, Frank. *The Lonely Voice: A Study of the Short Story.* Cleveland: World, 1963.

Peden, William. *The American Short Story: Continuity and Change, 1940—1975.* 2nd ed. Boston: Houghton Mifflin, 1975. A thorough survey of many genres and subgenres of short fiction.

Podhoretz, Norman. *Doings and Undoings: The Fifties and After in American Writing.* New York: Farrar, Straus, 1964. Includes discussion of O'Hara, McCarthy, Bellow, Baldwin, and Updike.

Ross, Danforth. *The American Short Story.* Minneapolis: University of Minnesota Pamphlets on American Literature, 1961.

Rubin, Louis D., and Jacobs, Robert D. *South: Modern Southern Literature in its Cultural Setting.* Garden City, N.Y.: Doubleday, 1961. Includes discussion of R. P. Warren, Welty, and McCullers.

Rupp, Richard H. *Celebration in Postwar American Fiction: 1945—1967.* Coral Gables: University of Miami Press, 1970. Includes discussion of Cheever, Updike, Welty, O'Connor, Salinger, Malamud, and Bellow.

Simonini, Rinaldo C., Jr., ed. *Southern Writers: Appraisals In Our Time.* Charlottesville: University Press of Virginia, 1964. A collection of essays from a cultural-historical perspective.

Tanner, Tony. *City of Words: American Fiction, 1950—1970.* New York: Harper & Row, 1971. Includes discussions of Nabokov, Bellow, Purdy, Vonnegut, Barth, Updike, Roth, and Malamud. Although devoted to their novels, the book contains much that is relevant to these authors' stories.

Thurston, Jarvis et al. *Short Fiction Criticism: A Checklist of Interpretations Since 1925 of Stories and Novelettes (American, British, Continental), 1800—1958.* Denver: Swallow Press, 1960.

Voss, Arthur. *The American Short Story: A Critical Survey.* Norman: University of Oklahoma Press, 1973. A historical survey and synthesis.

Walker, Warren S. *Twentieth-Century Short Fiction Explication: Interpretations, 1900—1975, of Short Fiction Since 1800,* 3rd ed. Hamden, Conn. Shoe String Press, 1977.

West, Ray B., Jr. *The Short Story in America, 1900—1950.* Chicago: Regnery, 1952.

Articles and Books Devoted
to Specific Authors

Louis Auchincloss

Kane, Patricia. "Lawyers at the Top: The Fiction of Louis Auchincloss." *Critique* 7, no.
2 (1964—65): 36—46. Surveys Auchincloss's fictional world and the standards of
his characters.

John Barth

Bienstock, Beverly Gray. "Lingering on the Autognostic Verge: John Barth's *Lost in the
Funhouse.*" *Modern Fiction Studies* 19, no. 1 (1973): 69—78. Finds the book's unity
in the self's search for identity.

Gillespie, Gerald. "Barth's *Lost in the Funhouse:* Short Story Text in its Cyclic Context."
Studies in Short Fiction 12, no. 3 (1975): 223—30.

Kyle, Carol A. "The Unity of Anatomy: The Structure of Barth's *Lost in the Funhouse.*"
Critique 13, no. 3 (1972): 31—43. Uses Frye's concept of anatomy to explain unity
"in its inherent multiplicity."

Morrell, David. *John Barth: An Introduction.* University Park: Pennsylvania State
University Press, 1976. Traces the creative process for each of Barth's works.

Tharpe, Jac. *John Barth: The Comic Sublimity of Paradox.* Carbondale: Southern Illinois
University Press, 1974. Surveys the major works and their underlying
philosophy.

Weixlmann, Joe, and Weixlmann, Sher. "Barth and Barthelme Recycle the Perseus
Myth: A Study in Literary Ecology." *Modern Fiction Studies* 25, no. 2 (1979):
191—208. Works using the Perseus figure by both authors are cited to show
their differences.

Saul Bellow

Clayton, John Jacob. *Saul Bellow: In Defense of Man.* Bloomington: Indiana University
Press, 1968. Bellow is seen as a psychological novelist of affirmation who rejects
the impersonality of his contemporaries' work.

Cohen, Sarah Blacher. *Saul Bellow's Enigmatic Laughter.* Chicago: University of Illinois
Press, 1974. Emphasizes Bellow's use of comedy as a retaliation against despair.

Critique 3, no. 3 (1960). An all-Bellow/Styron issue with six essays and a bibliography.

Demarest, David, P., Jr. "The Theme of Discontinuity in Saul Bellow's Fiction: 'Looking for Mr. Green' and 'A Father-To-Be.'" *Studies in Short Fiction* 6, no. 2 (1969): 175—86. These stories are viewed as introductions to the theme of inconsistency in Bellow's overall vision.

Donoghue, Denis. "Bellow in Short." *Art International* 12 (1969): 59—60, 64. Contrasts *Mosby's Memoirs* with *Herzog.*

Epstein, Joseph. "Saul Bellow of Chicago." *New York Times Book Review,* May 9, 1971, pp. 4—16. Contains many thoughtful comments from Bellow on his work and literary position.

Fuchs, Daniel. "Saul Bellow and the Modern Tradition." *Contemporary Literature* 15, no. 1 (1974): 67—89. Provides a new definition of modernism, with Bellow as its major exponent.

Lippit, Noriko M. "A Perennial Survivor: Saul Bellow's Heroine in the Desert." *Studies in Short Fiction* 12, no. 3 (1975): 281—83. Surveys an atypical story from Bellow's canon.

Malin, Irving, ed. *Saul Bellow and the Critics.* New York: New York University Press, 1967. Thirteen essays, most tracing various themes through the canon.

————. *Saul Bellow's Fiction.* Carbondale: Southern Illinois University Press, 1969. An easy-to-read book, divided into sections ("The Themes," "The Images," and so on).

Modern Fiction Studies 25, no. 1 (1979). An all-Bellow issue with eleven articles and a bibliography.

Opdahl, Keith Michael. *The Novels of Saul Bellow: An Introduction.* University Park: Pennsylvania State University Press, 1967. Treats psychological and social issues raised by Bellow.

Pinsker, Sanford. "Saul Bellow in the Classroom." *College English* 34 (1973): 975—82. Coverage of a Bellow lecture, contains analyses by Bellow.

Porter, M. Gilbert. *Whence the Power? The Artistry and Humanity of Saul Bellow.* Columbia: University of Missouri Press, 1974. Surveys the novels through *Mr. Sammler's Planet.*

Rovit, Earl, ed. *Saul Bellow: A Collection of Critical Essays.* Englewood Cliffs, N.J.: Prentice-Hall, 1975. Twelve essays, some literary biography, some treatments of individual works, others tracing ideas through multiple works.

Paul Bowles

Stewart, Lawrence Delbert. *Paul Bowles: The Illumination of North Africa.* Carbondale: Southern Illinois University Press, 1974.

Stanley Elkin

LeClair, Thomas. "The Obsessional Fiction of Stanley Elkin." *Contemporary Literature* 16, no. 2 (1975): 145—62. Includes discussion of his two volumes of short fiction.

Sanders, Scott. "An Interview with Stanley Elkin." *Contemporary Literature* 16, no. 2 (1975): 131—45. Elkin discusses his work, his penchant for extremes, and his debt to Faulkner and Gass.

George Garrett

Broughton, Irv, ed. "In Appreciation of George Garrett." Seattle: *Mill Mountain Review,* 1971. Articles, essays, and personal reminiscences.

William H. Gass

Bassoff, Bruce. "The Sacrificial World of William Gass: *In the Heart of the Heart of the Country.*" *Critique* 18, no. 1 (1976): 36—58. Surveys the book's thematic and symbolic unities.

Kane, Patricia. "The Sun Burned on the Snow: Gass's 'The Pedersen Kid.'" *Critique* 14, no. 2 (1972): 89—97. Discusses how the story is a unique variation on the initiation theme.

Caroline Gordon

Critique 1, no. 1 (1956). Issue devoted exclusively to Gordon contains six essays and a bibliography.

Rubin, Larry. "Christian Allegory in Caroline Gordon's 'The Captive.'" *Studies in Short Fiction* 5, no. 3 (1968): 283—89. Examines Calvinist elements in one of Gordon's early stories.

Stuckey, W. J. *Caroline Gordon.* New York: Twayne, 1972.

Shirley Ann Grau

Berland, Alwyn. "The Fiction of Shirley Ann Grau." *Critique* 6, no. 1 (1963): 78—84. Surveys three collections of stories.

Pearson, Ann. "Shirley Ann Grau: Nature Is the Vision." *Critique* 17, no. 2 (1975): 47—58. Discusses the influences of a natural setting on thematic purpose.

William Goyen

Phillips, Robert. *William Goyen.* Boston: Twayne, 1979. Contains chapters on *Ghost and Flesh, The Faces of Blood Kindred,* and *The Collected Stories.*

Langston Hughes

Emmanuel, James A. *Langston Hughes.* New York: Twayne, 1967.

Shirley Jackson

Friedman, Lenejmaja. *Shirley Jackson.* Boston: Twayne, 1975.

Bernard Malamud

Astro, Richard, and Benson, Jackson J., *The Fiction of Bernard Malamud.* Corvallis: Oregon State University Press, 1977. Seven essays and a bibliography, includes Ihab Hassan and Leslie Fiedler.

Avery, Evelyn Gross. *Rebels and Victims: The Fiction of Richard Wright and Bernard Malamud.* Port Washington, N.Y.: Kennikat Press, 1979. Covers the overlapping and contrasting attitudes toward suffering of black and Jewish characters.

Bellman, Samuel Irving. "Women, Children, and Idiots First: The Transformation Psychology of Bernard Malamud." *Critique* 7, no. 2 (1964—65): 123—38. Discusses what Bellman calls "Malamud's partial Judaization of society."

Ducharme, Robert. *Art and Ideas in the Novels of Bernard Malamud.* The Hague: Mouton, 1974. Divided into thematic subdivisions: myth, irony, suffering, family, and history.

Field, Leslie A., and Field, Joyce W., eds. *Bernard Malamud: A Collection of Critical Essays.* Englewood Cliffs, N.J.: Prentice-Hall, 1975. Eleven varied essays.

———. *Bernard Malamud and the Critics.* New York: New York University Press, 1970. Contains twenty-one essays in four areas: "In the Jewish Tradition?"; "Myth, Ritual, Folklore"; "Varied Approaches"; and "Specific Novels and Stories."

Goldman, Mark. "Bernard Malamud's Comic Vision and the Theme of Identity." *Critique* 7, no. 2 (1964—65): 92—109. Disagrees with Rovit; discusses affirmation and the search for identity.

Perrine, Lawrence. "Malamud's 'Take Pity.'" *Studies in Short Fiction* 2, no. 1 (1964): 84—86. Establishes the story's ambiguous setting from textual references.

Richman, Sidney. *Bernard Malamud.* New York: Twayne, 1966. Contains a chapter on the stories.

Rovit, Earl. "Bernard Malamud and the Jewish Literary Tradition." *Critique* 3, no. 2 (1959): 3—10. Discusses Malamud's self-conscious relation to the tradition.

James A. Michener
Day, A. Grove. *James Michener.* Boston: Twayne, 1977.

Vladimir Nabokov
Appel, Alfred, Jr. "An Interview with Vladimir Nabokov." *Wisconsin Studies in Contemporary Literature* 8, no. 2(1967):127—52. A wide-ranging interview in which Nabokov discusses criticism, Joyce, and details in his own work.

Fowler, Douglas. *Reading Nabokov.* New York: Cornell University Press, 1974. Limited, but useful as an introduction.

Lee, L. L. "Duplexity in V. Nabokov's Short Stories." *Studies in Short Fiction* 2, no. 4(1965):307—15. Discusses Nabokov's use of doubles, mirror imagery, and multiple levels of meaning.

———. *Vladimir Nabokov.* Boston: Twayne, 1976. Chapters two, eight, and nine are relevant to Nabokov's short works.

Modern Fiction Studies 25, no. 3 (1979). An all-Nabokov issue, including eight articles, three reviews, and a bibliography.

Rowe, William Woodin. *Nabokov's Deceptive World.* New York: New York University Press, 1971. Although devoted to the novels, this book contains much worthwhile discussion of Nabokov's linguistic technique, explicating many passages.

Stegner, Page. *Escape into Aesthetics: The Art of Vladimir Nabokov.* New York: Dial, 1966. Part One (chapters one, two, and three) is an overview of his career and works and is thus relevant to the short stories.

Williams, Carol T. "Nabokov's Dozen Short Stories: His World in Microcosm." *Studies in Short Fiction* 12, no. 3(1975):213—22. Nabokov's short fiction is about the "quest to unify the two worlds of the mundane and the ecstatic."

Joyce Carol Oates

Barza, Steven. "Joyce Carol Oates: Naturalism and the Aberrant Response." *Studies in American Fiction* 7, no. 2(1979):141—53. In the relationship between stimulus and response, Oates creates a contemporary naturalism.

Creighton, Joanne V. *Joyce Carol Oates.* Boston: Twayne, 1979. Chapter six deals exclusively with the short stories.

Friedman, Ellen G. *Joyce Carol Oates.* New York: Frederick Ungar, 1980. Treats the short stories only in passing.

Grant, Mary Kathryn. *The Tragic Vision of Joyce Carol Oates.* Durham, N.C.: Duke University Press, 1978. A survey of Oates's work from 1963 to 1973. Discusses her vision of violence and her theory of art.

Park, Sue Simpson. "A Study in Counterpoint: Joyce Carol Oates' 'How I Contemplated the World from the Detroit House of Correction and Began My Life Over Again.'" *Modern Fiction Studies* 22, no. 2(1976):213—24. Shows how the story's structure attempts to recreate the experiencing mind.

Pinsker, Sanford. "Joyce Carol Oates in the New Naturalism." *Southern Review* 15, no. 1(1979):52—63. Surveys affinities between naturalism (Pizar's definition) and Oates.

Wagner, Linda W., ed. *Critical Essays on Joyce Carol Oates.* Boston: Hall, 1979.

Walker, Carolyn. "Fear, Love, and Art in Oates' 'Plot.'" *Critique* 15, no. 1(1973):59—70. Discusses how fear contributes to the story's structure.

Waller, G. F. *Dreaming America: Obsession and Transcendence in the Fiction of Joyce Carol Oates.* Baton Rouge: Louisiana State University Press, 1979. Devoted mainly to the novels but includes discussion of themes relevant to the short stories.

Flannery O'Connor

Asals, Frederick. "The Mythic Dimensions of Flannery O'Connor's 'Greenleaf.'" *Studies in Short Fiction* 5, no. 4(1968):317—330. Discusses a symbology "of divine harmony."

Browning, Preston M., Jr. "Flannery O'Connor and the Demonic." *Modern Fiction Studies* 11, no. 1(1973):29—42. "Miss O'Connor seems to say that, in a time so well adjusted to itself that reflection becomes superfluous, the only way to the Holy is through the Demonic."

————. "'Parker's Back': Flannery O'Connor's Iconography of Salvation by Profanity." *Studies in Short Fiction* 6, no. 5(1969):525—35. Discusses O'Connor's treatment of fate and free will.

Coles, Robert. "Flannery O'Connor: A Southern Intellectual." *Southern Review* 16, no. 1(1980):46—64. Discusses pride and intellectualism in her work and life.

Doxey, William S. "A Dissenting Opinion of Flannery O'Connor's 'A Good Man is Hard to Find.'" *Studies in Short Fiction* 10, no. 2(1973):199—204. Doxey believes that this story is flawed by a superfluous shift in point of view.

Drake, Robert. "The Paradigm of Flannery O'Connor's True Country." *Studies in Short Fiction* 6, no. 4(1969):433—42. Views O'Connor's settings as microcosms in the tradition of Faulkner's Yoknapatawpha county and Hardy's Wessex.

Driskell, Leon V., and Brittain, Joan T. *The Eternal Crossroads: The Art of Flannery O'Connor.* Lexington: University Press of Kentucky, 1971. Chapters five and six are devoted to the short stories.

Edenstein, Mark G. "Flannery O'Connor and the Problem of Modern Satire." *Studies in Short Fiction* 12, no. 2(1975):139—44. Views O'Connor as a satirist.

Eggenschwiler, David. *The Christian Humanism of Flannery O'Connor.* Detroit: Wayne State University Press, 1972. The author argues that O'Connor "consistently wrote from the point of view of a Christian humanist."

Friedman, Melvin J., and Lawson, Lewis A. *The Added Dimension: The Art and Mind of Flannery O'Connor.* New York: Fordham University Press, 1977. Includes eleven diverse essays and a bibliography.

Kane, Patricia. "Flannery O'Connor's 'Everything that Rises must Converge.'" *Critique* 8 no. 1(1965):85—91. This review provides an excellent overview of the volume.

Maida, Patricia Dinneen. "Convergence in Flannery O'Connor's 'Everything that Rises must Converge.'" *Studies in Short Fiction* 7, no. 4(1970):549—55. Discusses the function of the book's title.

————. "Light and Enlightenment in Flannery O'Connor's Fiction." *Studies in Short Fiction* 13, no. 1(1976):31—36.

Marks, W. S., III. "Advertisements for Grace: Flannery O'Connor's 'A Good Man Is Hard to Find.'" *Studies in Short Fiction* 4, no. 1(1966):19—27. An allegorical approach that views her in the Hawthorne tradition.

Martin, Carter W. *The True Country: Themes in the Fiction of Flannery O'Connor.* Nashville: Vanderbilt University Press, 1969. A study of Christian themes and the "thematic significance of her use of symbolism, the grotesque, humor, and irony."

Milder, Robert. "The Protestantism of Flannery O'Connor." *Southern Review* 11, no. 4(1975):802—19. Milder's thesis is that "this most aggressively Catholic of American writers" produced works "uncompromisingly Protestant in substance."

Montgomery, Marion. "Flannery O'Connor and the Jansenist Problem in Fiction." *Southern Review* 14, no. 3(1978):438—48. Discusses determinism in O'Connor's works.

————. "On Flannery O'Connor's 'Everything that Rises must Converge.'" *Critique* 13, no. 2(1971):15—29. Discusses character of Julian in this story.

Orvell, Miles. *Invisible Parade: The Fiction of Flannery O'Connor.* Philadelphia: Temple University Press, 1972. Chapter four deals exclusively with the short stories.

Shinn, Thelma J. "Flannery O'Connor and the Violence of Grace." *Contemporary Literature* 9, no. 1(1968):58—73. Discusses how violence is used as a vehicle for redemption.

Shloss, Carol. *Flannery O'Connor's Dark Comedies: The Limits of Influence.* Baton Rouge: Louisiana State University Press, 1980. Discusses rhetorical devices and their significance.

Tate, J. C. "Flannery O'Connor's Counterplot." *Southern Review* 16, no. 4(1980):869—78. An interesting comparison of O'Connor's relationship with evil with Milton's relationship with Satan in *Paradise Lost.*

John O'Hara

Carson, Edward Russell. *The Fiction of John O'Hara.* Pittsburgh: University of Pittsburgh Press, 1961. Chapter three deals exclusively with the short stories.

Grebstein, Sheldon Norman. *John O'Hara.* New York: Twayne, 1966. Chapter five deals exclusively with the short stories.

O'Hara, John. *An Artist Is His Own Fault: John O'Hara on Writers and Writing.* Matthew J. Bruccoli, ed. Carbondale: Southern Illinois University Press, 1977. Forty-one lectures, essays, reviews, and interviews by O'Hara.

James Purdy

Schwarzschild, Bettina. *The Not-Right House: Essays on James Purdy.* Columbia: University of Missouri Press, 1968.

J. D. Salinger

French, Warren. *J. D. Salinger.* Boston: Twayne, 1976.

Goldstein, Bernice, and Goldstein, Sanford. "'Seymour: An Introduction'—Writing as Discovery." *Studies in Short Fiction* 7, no. 2(1970):248—256. Treats Salinger's focus on the process of creation through the character Buddy.

Modern Fiction Studies 12, no. 3(1966). An all-Salinger issue, including seven essays and a bibliography.

Perrine, Lawrence. "Teddy? Booper? or Blooper?" *Studies in Short Fiction* 4, no. 3(1967):217—224. A suggested interpretation of Salinger's ambiguous ending to this story.

William Saroyan

Floan, Howard R. *William Saroyan.* New York: Twayne, 1966.

Isaac Bashevis Singer

Alexander, Edward. *Isaac Bashevis Singer.* Boston: Twayne, 1980.

Allentuck, Marcie, ed. *The Achievement of Isaac Bashevis Singer.* Carbondale. Southern Illinois University Press, 1969.

Anderson, David M. "Isaac Bashevis Singer: Conversations in California." *Modern Fiction Studies* 16, no. 4(1970—71):423—40. A very articulate and informative interview with Singer.
Bezanker, Abraham. "I. B. Singer's Crises of Identity." *Critique* 14, no. 2(1972):71—88. Uses Erik Erikson's theories to explain problems in Singer.
Buchen, Irving H. "Isaac Bashevis Singer and the Eternal Past." *Critique* 8, no. 3(1966):5—18. Emphasizes the universality of Singer and the Yiddish tradition.
————. *Isaac Bashevis Singer and the Eternal Past.* New York: New York University Press, 1968. Emphasizes the universality of Singer and the Yiddish tradition.
Kresh, Paul. *Isaac Bashevis Singer: The Magician of West 86th Street.* New York: Dial, 1979.
Malin, Irving, ed. *Critical Views of Isaac Bashevis Singer.* New York: New York University Press, 1969.
Pinsker, Sanford. "The Fictive Worlds of Isaac Bashevis Singer." *Critique* 11, no. 2(1968):26—39. Discusses *Gimpel the Fool.*
————. "Isaac Bashevis Singer: An Interview." *Critique* 11, no. 2(1968):16—25. Singer discusses his goals and the process of translation.
Pondrom, Cyrena N. "Isaac Bashevis Singer: An Interview and a Biographical Sketch." *Contemporary Literature* 10, no. 1(1969):1—38. A broad, open interview and a chronology of his works.
————. "Isaac Bashevis Singer: An Interview, Part II." *Contemporary Literature* 10, no. 3(1969):331—51. Discusses stories in *Short Friday.*
Siegel, Ben. "Sacred and Profane: Isaac Bashevis Singer's Embattled Spirits." *Critique* 6, no. 1(1963):24—47. Discusses characters, themes, and the tradition, including *Gimpel the Fool.*
Zatlin, Linda G. "The Themes of Isaac Bashevis Singer's Short Fiction." *Critique* 11, no. 2(1968):40—48. Discusses Singer's theology.

Wallace Stegner
Robinson, Forrest G., and Robinson, Margaret G. *Wallace Stegner.* Boston: Twayne, 1977.

Jesse Stuart
Blair, Everetta Love. *Jesse Stuart: His Life and Works.* Columbia: University of South Carolina Press, 1967. Chapter three is devoted to the short stories.
Foster, Ruel E. *Jesse Stuart.* New York: Twayne, 1968. Chapter three is devoted to the short stories.

John Updike
Burehard, Rachael C. *John Updike: Yea Sayings.* Carbondale: Southern Illinois University Press, 1971.
Detweiler, Robert. *John Updike.* New York: Twayne, 1972.
Gado, Frank, ed. *First Person: Conversations on Writers & Writing.* Schenectady, N.Y.: Union College Press, 1973. Contains an informative 1970 interview with Updike.

Hunt, George W. *John Updike and the Three Great Secret Things: Sex, Religion, and Art.* Grand Rapids, Mich.: Eerdmans, 1980. Covers the religious and philosophical foundations of Updike's work.

Markle, Joyce B. *Fighters and Lovers: Themes in the Novels of John Updike.* New York: New York University Press, 1973.

Modern Fiction Studies 20, no. 1(1974). An all-Updike issue, including eight essays, three reviews, and a bibliography.

Oates, Joyce Carol. "Updike's American Comedies." *Modern Fiction Studies* 21, no. 3(1975):459—72. Discusses Updike's use of comedy, character types, and love.

Taylor, Larry E. *Pastoral and Anti-Pastoral Patterns in John Updike's Fiction.* Carbondale: Southern Illinois University Press, 1971.

Thornburn, David, and Eiland, Howard. *John Updike: A Collection of Critical Essays.* Englewood Cliffs, N.J.: Prentice-Hall, 1979. Contains articles on *The Same Door, Pigeon Feathers, The Music School, Bech: A Book,* and *Museums and Women.*

Robert Penn Warren

Bohner, Charles H. *Robert Penn Warren.* New York: Twayne, 1965.

Eudora Welty

Appel, Alfred, Jr. *A Season of Dreams: The Fiction of Eudora Welty.* Baton Rouge: Louisiana State University Press, 1965. Close readings of many stories.

Curley, Daniel. "Eudora Welty and the Quandam Obstruction." *Studies in Short Fiction* 5, no. 3(1968):209—24. An interpretation of the story "A Still Moment."

Davis, Charles E. "The South in Eudora Welty's Fiction: A Changing World." *Studies in American Fiction* 3, no. 2(1975):199—210. Welty treats the transition between the old and new South by placing her emphasis on the individual.

Desmond, John F., ed. *A Still Moment: Essays on the Art of Eudora Welty.* Metuchen, N.J.: Scarecrow, 1978. Six of this book's ten selections are relevant to the short stories.

Dollarhide, Louis, and Abadie, Ann J., eds. *Eudora Welty: A Form of Thanks.* Jackson: University Press of Mississippi, 1979. Six of this book's seven selections are relevant to the short stories.

Howard, Zelma Turner. *The Rhetoric of Eudora Welty's Short Stories.* Jackson: University Press of Mississippi, 1973. Discusses narrative voice, semantics, rhetorical devices, and so on.

Jones, William M. "The Plot as Search." *Studies in Short Fiction* 5, no. 1(1967):37—43. Speculates as to Welty's creative method.

Kreyling, Michael. *Eudora Welty's Achievement of Order.* Baton Rouge: Louisiana State University Press, 1980. Contains separate chapters on the respective story volumes.

McDonald, W. U., Jr. "Eudora Welty's Revisions of 'A Piece of News.'" *Studies in Short Fiction* 7, no. 2(1970):232—47. An eye-opening study of the impact of minor revisions.

————. "Welty's 'Social Consciousness': Revisions of 'The Whistle.'" *Modern Fiction Studies* 16, no. 2(1970):193—97. Shows how revision between periodical and book publication heightens social consciousness.

Oppitz, Kurt. "Eudora Welty: The Order of a Captive Soul." *Critique* 7, no. 2(1964—65):79—91. Welty characters search for order through the soul.

Vande Kieft, Ruth M. *Eudora Welty.* New York: Twayne, 1962.

Welty, Eudora. "Words into Fiction." *Southern Review* 1, no. 3(1965):543—53. Discusses the writer's craft. Welty makes no specific references to any of her works.

Jessamyn West

Shivers, Alfred T. *Jessamyn West.* New York: Twayne, 1972.

Index

Betts, Doris, 28, 54-55, 78, 83
"Bicycles, Muscles, Cigarets" (Carver), 100
"Big and Little" (Singer), 66
"Bill" (Powers), 97
Black Angels (Friedman), 70-71
Black Prince and Other Stories, The (Grau), 28
"Blackberry Winter" (Warren), 26
Blacks, stories of, 32-33, 35, 55-57
"Bleeding Heart, The" (Stafford), 8
Bloodline (Gaines), 55-56
Bloodshed and Three Novellas (Ozick), 99
"Blue Bottle, The" (Bradbury), 84
Blue Sash, and Other Stories, The (Beck), 15
"Blue-Winged Teal, The" (Stegner), 15
Booth, Wayne C., 80
Borrowed Summer and Other Stories (Enright), 14
Bowles, Paul, 78, 91-92
"Box of Ginger, A" (Calisher), 5
Boyle, Kay, 13-14
Bradbury, Ray, 2, 32, 70, 78, 84
"Brain Damage" (Barthelme), 80
Breakfast at Tiffany's: A Short Novel and Three Stories (Capote), 24
Breathing Trouble (Busch), 99
Bride of the Innisfallen and Other Stories, The (Welty), 19, 20
Brigadier and the Golf Widow, The (Cheever), 39, 40
"Brilliant Leaves, The" (Gordon), 28
"Burning, The" (Welty), 19
Busch, Frederick, 78, 99-100
By the North Gate (Oates), 86

"Cadence" (Dubus), 102
Calisher, Hortense, 5-6, 35, 49, 50-51
"Can You Carry Me?" (O'Hara), 3

Cape Cod Lighter, The (O'Hara), 48
Capote, Truman, 1, 22-24
"Captain's Son, The" (Taylor), 106
Carver, Raymond, 78, 86, 100
Cassill, R. V., 51
Cast a Cold Eye (McCarthy), 7
Cat on a Hot Tin Roof (Williams), 24
Catcher in the Rye, The (Salinger), 10
"Caveat Emptor" (Stafford), 70
Chase, Richard, 36
Cheever, John, 35, 36-40
Children Are Bored on Sunday (Stafford), 8
Children Is All (Purdy), 69
"Chip Canary" (Kentfield), 52
"Chip off the Old Block" (Stegner), 15
"Christmas Gift" (Warren), 26
"Christmas Memory, A" (Capote), 24
"Chronicle of Love, A" (Francis), 93
"Circle of Light" (Shaw), 49
Circus in the Attic, The (Warren), 25, 26
"City Boy" (Michaels), 95-96
"City Life" (Barthelme), 79, 80
City of the Living, The (Stegner), 15
"City Was in Total Darkness, The" (Shaw), 12
"Claims Artist, The" (Hall), 86
"Clay Wars, The" (Targan), 105
Clayton, John Bell, 54
Clearing in the Sky and Other Stories (Stuart), 29
Cold Ground Was My Bed Last Night (Garrett), 54
Collected Stories (Van Doren), 14
Collected Stories of Hortense Calisher, The, 51
Color of Darkness (Purdy), 69
Come Back, Dr. Caligari (Barthelme), 79
"Comforts of Home, The" (O'Connor), 68
"Comic Strip" (Garrett), 54

Enormous Radio and Other Stories, The (Cheever), 37
Enright, Elizabeth, 14
"Envy" (Ozick), 99
Erskine, Albert, 49
"Escape Artist, The" (O'Connor), 102
Everything that Rises must Converge (O'Connor), 54, 66-69, 97
Experimental stories, 75, 77, 108-109
Extreme Magic (Calisher), 50

Faces of Blood Kindred, The (Goyen), 53
"Faithful, The" (McPherson), 95
"Fancy Woman, The" (Taylor), 17
"Far from the City of Class" (Friedman), 70-71
Far Whistle, and Other Stories, The (Beck), 15
Farrell, James T., 1, 29
Father, The (Cassill), 51
Faulkner, William, 16
Fencing Master, The (Rogin), 49
"Field of Blue Children, The" (Williams), 24
"Field of Snow on a Slope of the Rosenberg, A" (Davenport), 90
Fifteen by Three (anthology), 85
Files on Parade (O'Hara), 2
First Fish, and Other Stories, The (Beck), 15
First Lover and Other Stories (Boyle), 13
"First Seven Years, The" (Malamud), 58
"Fitified Man" (Stuart), 29
"Fling, The" (Carver), 100
"For Esmé—with Love and Squalor" (Salinger), 11
Forest of the South, The (Gordon), 27-28
"Forever and the Earth" (Bradbury), 84
"Forks, The" (Power), 9

"Fortune of Arleus Kane, The" (Auchincloss), 6
"Frame-Tale" (Barth), 73
Francis, H. E., 78, 92-93
Franny and Zooey (Salinger), 11
"Free" (O'Hara), 3
French Girls are Vicious and Other Stories (Farrell), 29
Friedman, Bruce J., 70-71
Friend of Kafka and Other Stories, A (Singer), 98
Friendly Persuasion, The (West), 30
"Frog-Trouncin' Contest" (Stuart), 29

Gaines, Ernest, 55-56
"Gambler: A Portrait of the Writer, The" (Hall), 86
"Garden, The" (Bowles), 92
Garrett, George, 54
Gass, William H., 51, 52-53
Gentle Insurrection and Other Stories, The (Betts), 28
"Gentleman from Cracow, The" (Singer), 65
"Geranium, The" (O'Connor), 97
"Gesturing" (Updike), 108
Ghost and Flesh: Stories and Tales (Goyen), 15-16, 53-54
"Gift Bearer, The" (O'Connor), 102
Gimpel the Fool (Singer), 63, 65
"Girls in Their Summer Dresses, The" (Shaw), 12, 89
"Giving Blood" (Updike), 43
Glass Menagerie, The (Williams), 24
"Glass Mountain, The" (Barthelme), 79
"Goal of Life is Death, The" (Busch), 100
God Was Here But He Left Early (Shaw), 89